# So You Think You Know London?

## Clive Gifford

a division of Hodder Headline Limited

*To Fay, Geoff, Peter and Michelle Thompson,*
*for their friendship and support*

© Hodder Children's Books 2004

Published in Great Britain in 2004
by Hodder Children's Books

Editor: Gill Munton
Design by Fiona Webb
Cover design: Hodder Children's Books

The right of Clive Gifford to be identified as the author
of the work has been asserted by him in accordance
with the Copyright, Designs and Patents Act 1988.

10 9 8 7 6 5 4 3 2 1

ISBN: 0-340-88189-5

Printed by Bookmarque Ltd, Croydon, Surrey

Hodder Children's Books
a division of Hodder Headline Limited
338 Euston Road
London NW1 3B

# Contents

# Introduction

So you think you know all there is to know about England's capital city - its history, its people, its triumphs and its tragedies? You reckon you can recall all its famous sights and sounds, its landmarks, its transport system and its curiosities?

In this book you will find a whopping (or should that be Wapping?) 1,050 questions on all sorts of topics related to London - from its tallest buildings to its deepest underground tunnels, from its greatest heroes to its most notorious villains. Whether or not you know your Buckingham Palace from your Crystal Palace and your Blackfriars from your Whitechapel, this book should provide you with a real challenge - and you may pick up some fascinating facts about this magical city in the process.

## About the author

Clive Gifford was born on the outskirts of London, and lived and worked in the city for ten years before moving to Manchester. Clive has frolicked in the fountain in Trafalgar Square, played softball in Regent's Park, and been frightened out of his wits in the London Dungeons. In between visits to London, Clive has written more than 50 non-fiction books for adults and children, including all the books in the *So You Think You Know ...* quiz series. Other titles in this series feature questions based on Harry Potter, the Lord of the Rings, the Simpsons, and the 1960s, 1970s and 1980s.

# London for beginners

1. What is the name of London's major river?

2. What is the nickname, beginning with 't', of the London Underground system?

3. Name the largest and busiest of the airports which serve London.

4. What colour are the uniforms of London's police officers?

5. Which building is the official London home of the King or Queen of England?

6. Are the Houses of Parliament in Aldwych, Holborn, Bloomsbury or Westminster?

7. What colour are most of London's buses?

8. London celebrates with fireworks and bonfires on which day of November?

9. Most of the London Underground track is above ground: true or false?

10. Which London football club has its home ground at Stamford Bridge?

11. What is the name of the street which is famous for its fashion and music shops and which has Tottenham Court Road underground station at one end?

12. Name the west London carnival which occurs each year on the August Bank Holiday weekend.

13. In which colour is the Northern Line shown on maps of the London Underground?

14. Which major international tennis tournament is held in south London each June?

15. How many trips are made on the London Underground every year: over 500 million, over 800 million or over 1,000 million?

16. Which bird is found throughout London, but in especially large numbers in Trafalgar Square?

17. What colour are London's post boxes?

18. Would you find Big Ben in Leicester Square, Trafalgar Square, Westminster or Buckingham Palace?

19. On which London Underground line are the stations Covent Garden, Knightsbridge and Hatton Cross?

20. In which direction does the River Thames flow: east, north or west?

21. The Beatles were born and grew up in London: true or false?

22. What is the name given to the area of London famous for its theatres?

23. If you walked from Westminster Cathedral to Buckingham Palace, in which compass direction would you be heading?

24. Buckingham Palace has its own swimming pool and cinema: true or false?

25. Is the London Planetarium on Charing Cross Road, Museum Street, Marylebone Road or Regent Street?

26. Which of these London Underground stations is not at one end of the Victoria Line: Brixton, Walthamstow Central or Pimlico?

27. Who currently lives in Buckingham Palace: Queen Elizabeth II, Prince Charles, Princess Anne or Prince Edward?

28. If you travelled from Morden in south London to Leicester Square in the city centre, which London Underground line would you use?

29. Which sport is played at the Oval in south London?

30. What number Downing Street is the home of the British Prime Minister?

31. What colour is the door of the British Prime Minister's home?

32. Give the names of two London Underground stations which contain the word 'court'.

33. London's famous waxworks museum is named after which lady?

34. Which tall structure stands in the middle of Trafalgar Square?

35. Which word needs to be added to each of the following to complete the names of three underground stations: Willesden, Golders, Turnham and Wood?

36. Near which 'circus' would you find the Trocadero: Oxford Circus, Piccadilly Circus or Cambridge Circus?

37. Which London museum is famous for its skeletons of giant dinosaurs?

38. Which of these counties does not border Greater London: Surrey, Essex, Dorset or Kent?

39. Which historic building, west of central London, is famous for its large maze?

40. Which sport is played at Upton Park in east London: football, basketball, cricket or rugby?

41. A statue of which children's book character stands in Hyde Park: Alice in Wonderland, Peter Pan, Paddington Bear or SuperTed?

42. Which historic building is guarded by Beefeaters?

43. How many times has London hosted the Olympic Games?

44. Which invaders founded London as a permanent settlement: the Ancient Celts, the Romans, the Ancient Greeks or the Vikings?

45. Find a London Underground station with the word 'white' in its name.

46. In which century did the Great Fire of London devastate the city?

47. Which structure was built in Greenwich to commemorate the approach of the 21st century?

48. Aircraft from which country bombed London during the Blitz in the Second World War?

49. If you were looking at soldiers in red uniforms with large black hats swapping duties outside Buckingham Palace, which ceremony would you be viewing?

50. Britney Spears' waxwork at Madame Tussaud's holds the record for being on display for the shortest time before being melted down: true or false?

# Royal London

1. Who had the longest reign of all the British kings and queens?

2. In which church were Prince Charles and Lady Diana Spencer married?

3. In which season of the year is the State Opening of Parliament performed by the current king or queen?

4. In which church have England's kings and queens been crowned for over 900 years?

5. In which building are the Crown Jewels?

6. Who was the British monarch before Queen Elizabeth II?

7. Queen Elizabeth II was born on 21 April, but in which month is her official birthday?

8. A statue of which king, famous for leading crusades, stands outside the Houses of Parliament?

9. How many different regiments of soldiers are involved in the Changing of the Guard ceremonies outside Buckingham Palace?

10. Which king bought Buckingham Palace and turned it into the official London residence for the monarch in 1762?

11. Who lived in Clarence House until her death in 2002?

12. Which major ceremony is held in London on the second Saturday in June every year, drawing large crowds of tourists?

13. Which palace was the residence of Princess Diana?

14. In which royal residence, to the west of London, does the Queen often stay in the summer?

15. Which English king caused a split, which exists to this day, in the Christian church?

16. Which royal residence in London shows its back to the public?

17. From which palace did Queen Elizabeth II make her first speech as Queen: St James's Palace, Buckingham Palace or Kensington Palace?

18. The Trooping of the Colour involves the Queen travelling from Buckingham Palace to which parade ground?

19. How much did King George III pay for Buckingham Palace: £28,000, £280,000, £2.8 million or £28 million?

20. What is the official name of the tall black furry hat worn by a Palace guard on duty?

21. By which name are the Yeoman Warders at the Tower of London better known?

22. Which annual ceremony, attended by members of the Royal Family, is held on the Sunday nearest to 11 November?

23. Which English king was confined in St James's Palace before his execution in 1649?

24. What is the name of the wide road which links Buckingham Palace to Trafalgar Square?

25. Who was Queen Victoria's husband?

26. Which London museum was called 'The Museum of Manufactures' and, later, 'The South Kensington Museum', before acquiring its current title?

27. When the Royal Standard flag flies above Buckingham Palace, what does it tell the outside world?

28. William III and Mary II bought Nottingham House in what was then the village of Kensington, and transformed it into which palace?

29. Who was the first king to live in Hampton Court Palace?

30. Hyde Park was originally land taken over by Henry VIII from which church?

31. In which year were the State Rooms of Buckingham Palace first opened to the public?

32. Which of the following is not a royal park: Regent's Park, Holland Park, Green Park or Hyde Park?

33. Which Tudor monarch established the Woolwich weapons and ammunition depot which later became known as the Royal Arsenal?

34. The Festival of Remembrance features a gun salute, a two-minute silence and wreaths laid at the base of which memorial?

35. Which of the following were executed at the Tower of London: Anne Boleyn, Mary I, Lady Jane Grey and Henry VII?

36. Was King Edward VII born in Buckingham Palace, St James's Palace, Windsor Castle or Kensington Palace?

37. Who opened parts of Kensington Palace on her 80th birthday in 1898?

38. Which house became the official residence of the Prince of Wales in 1850, but is now known as the Commonwealth Centre?

39. Buckingham Palace's grounds include gardens of over 45 acres and a heliport: true or false?

40. What does the Queen distribute to a number of senior citizens of London on Maundy Thursday?

41. In which House does the monarch sit on a throne and read out the Government's plans for new laws during the State Opening of Parliament?

42. Where does the King's Troop of the Royal Horse Artillery fire a gun salute on the Queen's official birthday?

43. The Mounting the Guard ceremony usually involves which of these regiments: the Household Cavalry, the Grenadier Guards or the Coldstream Guards?

44. Are the Royal Mews near Buckingham Palace used to house the monarch's servants, the state carriages and horses, or the Royal Family's art collection?

45. Was William the Conqueror crowned in 1066, 1067, 1118 or 1132?

46. Princess Augusta founded which large botanic gardens in south-west London?

47. Which building stands on the site of the ancient palace of kings and queens used by Edward the Confessor and William I?

48. Which ceremony takes place at 9.53 p.m. every evening at the Tower of London?

49. Until 1754, the Royal Family demonstrated its humility on Maundy Thursday when the monarch (or an aide) had to perform a task. Was this task to cook a meal for an ordinary family, to wash the feet of the poor, or to do a day's work on a farm?

50. In which year was Queen Victoria crowned: 1800, 1827 or 1837?

# Olde London

1. Who invaded Britain in 43 AD?

2. The remains of an Iron Age fort – and a windmill in which Lord Baden-Powell is believed to have written his Boy Scout manual – can be found on a London common. Is it Wimbledon Common, Putney Common or Clapham Common?

3. Who brought the first printing press to England when he set up business in London in 1474?

4. How many people died in the Great Fire of London: 6, 60, 600 or 6,000?

5. Threadneedle Street is the location of which famous financial building?

6. The Banqueting House was the scene of the beheading of Charles I. In which London palace is it to be found: Whitehall Palace, Lambeth Palace, St James's Palace or Buckingham Palace?

7. Was London formerly known as Londinium, Thamestown, Windsorium or Angleville?

8. Hippos and rhinos once lived in the wild in the Thames Valley: true or false?

9. Which bridge was used for displaying the severed heads of traitors for a number of centuries?

10. A wall was built around London in 200 AD. Was it built by the Romans, the Celts, the Saxons or the Phoenicians?

11. Work on London's first stone bridge started in 1176. Until which century did it remain London's only bridge over the Thames?

12. An estimated 80,000 Londoners were killed in the 17th century by a devastating event. Was it the Great Fire of London, the Great Plague, or the Hundred Years War?

13. Which famous Tudor explorer was knighted by Queen Elizabeth I at Deptford after his round-the-world voyage?

14. Did Saxon, Viking or Norman traders once live in the area now known as Covent Garden?

15. Which famous road, which runs from Trafalgar Square to the City of London, used to be the beach of the River Thames?

16. For which one of these is Pudding Lane famous: the first signs of the Great Plague, London's first police station, or the beginning of the Great Fire of London?

17. How many Prime Ministers have been shot and killed in the House of Commons since 1751?

18. Was Tilbury Fort built by the Tudors, the Stuarts, the Normans or the Romans?

19. Followers of which religion were banished from London and the rest of Britain in 1290?

20. In what sort of food-making shop did the Great Fire of London break out in 1666?

21. In Roman times, did Ermine Street run from London to Canterbury, York or Winchester?

22. Which of the following was not a gate in the ancient wall built around London: Highgate, Bishopgate, Aldgate or Ludgate?

23. Where were the London Frost Fairs held?

24. Was St Bartholomew's Hospital founded in 1123, 1388, 1571 or 1702?

25. Were 17, 37, 57 or 87 churches destroyed in the Great Fire of London?

26. The nursery rhyme *Ring-a-Ring-o'-Roses* is based on an event that struck London in the 1660s. Which event was it?

27. 'One, London' is the postal address of the Duke of Wellington's former home, Apsley House: true or false?

28. Which famous Danish king managed to take control of London and much of England by 1017?

29. Which plague swept through London in the 14th century?

30. In Anglo-Saxon times, was London called Londinium, Lundenwic, Alde Wych or Ludfort?

31. Did Elephant and Castle take its name from a zoo that once stood there, an Arab merchant who once lived there, or a guild of craftsmen who made knife handles out of ivory?

32. Is Inderwick's of Carnaby Street England's oldest tailor's, pipe maker's or public house?

33. Which London market, whose name begins with the letter 's', was established as a horse fair by 1173?

34. When King Henry VIII came to power in 1509, was the population of London about 50,000, about 150,000, about 250,000, or about half a million?

35. Piccadilly was named after a kind of stiff collar made by tailors who lived in the area in the 17th century: true or false?

36. The assistant of the printer William Caxton relocated their printing press to which street, which later became famous for newspaper production?

37. The treasurer of which monarch was chased through London by an angry mob and beheaded with a bread knife: Edward II, Henry V or Elizabeth I?

38. Was the original St Paul's Cathedral built in 604, 892, 1089 or 1312?

39. Which animals were slaughtered in the mistaken belief that this would keep the Great Plague at bay?

40. Freibourg and Treyer on the Haymarket has been established since 1720. Does this shop sell snuff and tobacco, rope, swords or hats?

41. In Roman times, did Watling Street run from London to St Albans, Winchester or Nottingham?

42. Was William Caxton's first printing press set up in Southwark, Camden Town, Piccadilly or Westminster?

43. For how long has Arthur Beale, a shop on Shaftesbury Avenue, been selling rope and boating products: 200 years, 300 years, 400 years or 500 years?

44. How many years apart were the Great Plague and the Great Fire of London?

45. Which animals played a large part in the spreading of the plague that struck London in 1665?

46. Which great architect oversaw the rebuilding of some 50 of London's churches after the Great Fire of London?

47. Which London street used to be the site of docks: Oxford Street, Farringdon Street or Goodge Street?

48. Which religious sect celebrates the Spring Equinox in a ceremony on Tower Hill Terrace overlooked by the Tower of London: warlocks, Druids or witches?

49. On which side of the River Thames was the Roman settlement which later became known as London?

50. Was 1814 the date of the last Frost Fair, the last hanging in London, or the first London bus service?

# London transport

1. Which underground line will take you to Heathrow airport?

2. Harry Beck designed the world-famous London Underground map. Was he paid 5 guineas, 500 guineas or 5,000 guineas?

3. From which railway station does the Eurostar service to Europe run?

4. Which London Underground line is shown in light blue on the map?

5. What is the name of the motorway which encircles London?

6. Was London the first, second or third city in the world to open an underground railway?

7. Which London Underground line, taken over by British Rail in the 1990s, is the shortest, measuring just 2.22km in length: the Waterloo & City Line, the Bakerloo Line or the East London Line?

8. How many trips are made every weekday on London buses: 1.4 million, 3.4 million or 5.4 million?

9. London motorists pay over £330 million a year - in what?

10. Which of these London Underground lines has the most stations: the Piccadilly Line, the Central Line or the District Line?

11. What is the average distance travelled by a London Underground train in a year: 26,000 km, 49,000 km, 71,000 km or 118,000 km?

12. Which London Underground line is shown in green on the map?

13. A London taxi is available for hire if its yellow light is on: true or false?

14. Which two of the following London Underground lines have stations lying south of the River Thames: the East London Line, the Piccadilly Line, the Bakerloo Line and the Circle Line?

15. Only one London Underground escalator takes passengers up to the train platforms rather than down. Is it at Greenford, Earl's Court or Hendon?

16. Which airport is known by the abbreviation 'LGW'?

17. Between which two Piccadilly Line stations is the shortest tube journey in London, a distance of under 280 m?

18. Where is the larger of London's two National Express coach stations situated?

19. What is the name of the airport which is only 9.5 km away from the centre of London?

20. Which London Underground line is shown in silver on the map?

21. A London taxi driver must spend a year learning about the roads of London before gaining a licence. What is the name of this study?

22. Only one London Underground station has the name of an animal as part of its name. Which station is it?

23. Which motorway heads west out of London, starting from Chiswick?

24. Which of these London Underground stations is further west: Bethnal Green or Stratford?

25. Which of these stations has the most escalators: Leicester Square, King's Cross or Waterloo?

26. Two of London's main overground railway stations have the word 'Cross' in their names. Which stations are they?

27. Into how many fare zones is the London Underground divided?

28. Which London Underground line splits into two branches north of Camden Town?

29. How many terminals does London's Heathrow airport have?

30. At 74 km, which is the longest London Underground line?

31. The Metropolitan Line opened in 1863. Were its trains run on diesel, steam or electricity?

32. If you walked from Spitalfields Market to Smithfield Market, in which compass direction would you be heading?

33. What lies on the south bank of the Thames between Wandsworth Bridge and Battersea Bridge? (It is the only one of its kind in central London.)

34. What is the name of the world's busiest single-runway airport?

35. Which of these London Underground stations is furthest east: Queensway, Marble Arch or St Paul's?

36. Which two of these London Underground stations lie south of the River Thames: Bank, Rotherhithe, Gunnersbury, Vauxhall and Putney Bridge?

37. What is the name of the railway line which opened in 1987 with 15 stations and has since been expanded?

38. Which road runs along the eastern edge of Hyde Park between Marble Arch and Hyde Park Corner?

39. Is Gatwick, Heathrow or Stansted the closest airport to central London?

40. Which of these London Underground stations is furthest north: Warren Street, Tottenham Court Road or Leicester Square?

41. How long did it take Robert Robinson to visit every single London Underground station: nearly 19 hours, nearly 29 hours or nearly 31 hours?

42. Which of the following is not an abandoned tube station: Wood Lane, Down Street or Vauxhall Cross?

43. Which of these London Underground stations is the deepest: Hampstead, Aldgate or Blackfriars?

44. Which London Underground line is just 13.5 km long but carries over 175 million passengers every year?

45. Which tube station has the shallowest lift, carrying passengers just 9 metres: Chalk Farm, Chancery Lane or Covent Garden?

46. Earl's Court became the first station to install which device in 1911?

47. If you walked across Lambeth Bridge towards Southwark, in which compass direction would you be heading?

48. Which of these London Underground stations is furthest south: Southfields, Wimbledon Park or Fulham Broadway?

49. What is London's busiest tube station?

50. Which road runs, north of the Thames, from Westminster Bridge to Blackfriars?

# London crime

1. What is the name of London's police force?

2. What is the name given to its headquarters?

3. How many attempts were made on Queen Victoria's life: one, three, five or nine?

4. The phrase 'in the clink' (in prison) was coined in the days of the Clink Prison on the south bank of the River Thames: true or false?

5. Georgy Markov was murdered, allegedly by a secret agent, on Waterloo Bridge in 1978. Was the murder weapon a cigarette lighter, an umbrella, or a golf club which injected a lethal pellet?

6. Which one of these famous locations was not hit by a bomb planted by Irish nationalists in 1884-5: London Bridge, the Tower of London, Marble Arch, the House of Commons, or Scotland Yard?

7. In the 17th century, was a 'prigger of prancers' a street seller, a horse thief, a burglar or a pickpocket?

8. Which event took place for the last time in London at Newgate Prison in 1868?

9. Annie Chapman, Catherine Eddowes, Mary Jane Kelly and Elizabeth Stride were all victims of which murderer?

10. How many different crimes were punishable by death in London in the early 19th century: 6, 60, 114 or more than 300?

11. Which twin brothers ran an East End crime ring and were convicted of the murder of Jack 'The Hat' McVitie?

12. The Central Criminal Court, which serves the City of London, is better known by what name?

13. In 1530, Henry VIII legalised which one of the following punishments for women who murdered their husbands: boiling them in oil, cutting off their legs, skinning them alive, or drowning them?

14. In 1981, serious riots occurred in which south London district?

15. What event took place for many centuries at Tyburn (near the site where Marble Arch now stands)?

16. In 1963, the Glasgow to London Royal Mail train was robbed just north of London. What is the name given to this crime?

17. The first ever prisoner in the Tower of London, the Bishop of Durham, escaped by making his guards drunk and then using a rope: true or false?

18. The Richardson gang controlled much of the criminal activity in the 1950s - in south, north, east or west London?

19. Were the Bow Street Runners getaway drivers, the forerunners of the Metropolitan Police, or drug couriers?

20. What was the name of the call girl at the centre of the 1963 Profumo scandal?

21. In 1984, a bomb damaged which very famous department store in Knightsbridge?

22. At which carnival in 1976 was there a major riot which injured some 400 police officers?

23. 'Coppers' is a nickname for London police officers because the first police station was situated at Copthorne Street: true or false?

24. Who was the highwayman who was reputed to have ridden on horseback from London to York in under 24 hours?

25. In 1861, which illuminating feature was introduced to designate London police stations?

26. Which telephone number (introduced in 1937) should you dial to contact the police in an emergency?

27. Jack Addison had committed a number of highway robberies before he was executed in 1711. Was it 11, 23 or 56?

28. Which prison used to stand where the Central Criminal Court is now: Newgate, Pentonville, Highgate or Holloway?

29. How many people were reported to gather for public executions at Tyburn: 5,000, 10,000, 20,000 or 100,000?

30. In which historic London building were two young royal brothers murdered in the 15th century?

31. Which Great Train Robber made a sensational escape from Wandsworth Prison in 1965?

32. Where did all the murders involving the mysterious Jack the Ripper take place: the West End, the City of London, or the East End?

33. The Tyburn Tree used to stand at what is now the junction of Oxford Street, Park Lane and Edgware Road. How many people could be hung from its gallows in one go: 4, 6, 8 or 24?

34. How many London police officers were dismissed for drunkenness in 1823: 5, 12, 21 or 215?

35. In 1966, which spy escaped from a London prison?

36. Which one of the following was not one of the Great Train Robbers: Ronnie Biggs, Charlie Wilson, Jack Fenshaw or Thomas Wisbey?

37. Metropolitan Police Chief Inspector Dew raced across the Atlantic Ocean in 1910 to catch which murderer: Jack the Ripper, Dr Crippen, or the Stockwell Strangler?

38. In which year were women fully integrated into the Metropolitan Police: 1898, 1912, 1926 or 1973?

39. Which crime-fighting force was set up as the result of an Act of Parliament in 1829?

40. What fraction of prisoners in Newgate Prison during the 19th century survived to face their execution: $\frac{1}{4}$, $\frac{3}{4}$ or $\frac{9}{10}$ ?

41. Inside which London prison were executions carried out until 1961?

42. What was the name of the east London tower block whose corner flats collapsed in 1968?

43. Before she became Queen of England, Elizabeth I was imprisoned in the Tower of London - by her half-sister, her father or her uncle?

44. The television presenter Jill Dando was murdered outside her home in 1999. Was this in Fulham, Holborn, Hampstead or Islington?

45. For what small sum were Mill Hill, East Finchley and Hanwell cemeteries sold by Westminster Council in 1987?

46. Who was responsible for the formation of the Metropolitan Police Force: Sir Robert Peel, Benjamin Disraeli or Sir Horace Walpole?

47. What was the gruesome-sounding name of the man who attempted to steal the Crown Jewels from the Tower of London in 1671?

48. Police officer Keith Blakelock was killed in a frenzied attack which took place on the Broadwater Farm Estate in 1985. In which part of London is this estate?

49. Who was found guilty of shooting her lover outside a pub in Hampstead and became the last woman to be hanged in Britain?

50. The hangman at Tyburn was entitled to the clothes of the executed prisoners: true or false?

# London's Swinging 60s

1. Which street, between Regent Street and Oxford Street, became the home of the major new fashion movement in London during the 1960s?

2. Which famous jazz club moved its premises to Soho's Frith Street in 1965?

3. Who was the London hairstylist who became famous during the 1960s for his geometrical haircuts?

4. Which type of shop became legal in London in 1961?

5. Which famous music venue in Wardour Street helped to launch the careers of the Rolling Stones and many other sixties bands?

6. In which St John's Wood street were the EMI studios in which the Beatles recorded many of their albums?

7. Which Chelsea road attracted fashion trendsetters in the 1960s?

8. Which pop band were the first to have their likenesses displayed at Madame Tussaud's, an event which occurred in 1964?

9. In April 1963, 70,000 marchers demonstrated in London against nuclear weapons. Where had their march begun?

10. Which flower was used as a logo by the sixties designer Mary Quant?

11. Where was the large London festival at which the Rolling Stones played just two days after Brian Jones' death?

12. *Itchycoo Park* and *Lazy Sunday Afternoon* were hits for which popular London band?

13. Barbara Hulanicki opened which famous boutique in London during the 1960s?

14. The musical *Stop the World - I Want to Get Off* was co-written by and starred which London singer and actor?

15. London designer Mr Fish inspired the nickname of which item of clothing (it grew wider during the 1960s)?

16. Which singer, born in Stepney in the East End of London, started out in the sixties with the name David Jones?

17. Which ankle-high, elasticated item of footwear was named after a fashionable part of London?

18. What were first issued in London in 1960: parking tickets, premium bonds, or £50 notes?

19. Which band included the brothers Ray and Dave Davies, who were brought up in Hornsey in London?

20. What was the name of the dog who found the World Cup trophy in a south London garden in March 1966?

21. Sixties model Jean Shrimpton had a relationship with which famous fashion photographer from the East End?

22. Which district of London became notorious for its brothels and strip bars in the 1960s?

23. The Quorum boutique in Chelsea became famous for the work of which designer: Betsey Johnson, Anne Fogarty or Ossie Clark?

24. Which actor, born in Rotherhithe, starred in influential sixties films including *Alfie* and *The Ipcress File*?

25. Which model was born in Neasden as Lesley Hornby?

26. Rod Stewart went to the same London school as the lead members of the Kinks: true or false?

27. Which female London singer won the Eurovision Song Contest in 1967 with *Puppet on a String*?

28. What change to Londoners' home addresses was made in 1966?

29. Which of the following artists did not record in Denmark Street's Regent Sounds Studio during the 1960s: Simon and Garfunkel, the Rolling Stones or Jimi Hendrix?

30. Was Lord John the first boutique in Carnaby Street, Oxford Street, Soho or King's Road?

31. Number 3 Savile Row was the headquarters of the record company Apple in the late 1960s. Which famous band did it have on its books: the Rolling Stones, the Beatles or the Who?

32. Which famous American guitarist lived at 20 Manchester Square in London in 1969-70?

33. Which tube station was the first to have an automatic ticket barrier (in 1964): Stamford Brook, Hatton Cross, Pimlico or Leicester Square?

34. Which London-based playwright wrote *Loot* and *What The Butler Saw* before dying in 1967?

35. Three members of which band were arrested for urinating on the walls of an east London garage forecourt in 1965?

36. Which type of public transport had disappeared from London by the end of 1962?

37. What hit London in December 1962, causing more than 50 deaths?

38. What is the name of the island in the Thames on which many groups, including the Who and the Rolling Stones, played in the 1960s?

39. In which year did the Beatles play a lunchtime rooftop concert which resulted in a traffic jam?

40. Which London actor played the lead role in the 1960s musical *Half a Sixpence*: Joe Brown, Michael Caine, Sandie Shaw or Tommy Steele?

41. Which rock and pop venue moved from Oxford Street to Wardour Street in 1964?

42. Which London football team was the first to 'do the double' (win the English League championship and the FA Cup) in the 20th century?

43. Which London-based rhythm and blues band featured the guitarists Eric Clapton, Jimmy Page and Peter Green (at different times)?

44. Which dance, seen in London clubs during the early 1960s, was popularised by a Chubby Checker single?

45. The London County Council was replaced by which body in 1968?

46. Did Sir Terence Conran open his first Habitat store in Holborn, Fulham, Whitechapel or Islington?

47. Which Soho club, founded in 1962 by Peter Cook, played a major part in launching the satire boom of the 1960s?

48. Which television channel began broadcasting from London in 1964?

49. In 1967, Balham became the location of the first branch of which chain of inexpensive furniture stores?

50. Which London Underground line was opened in the 1960s: the Jubilee Line, the Victoria Line, or the Central Line?

# London at war

1. Hyde Park had its own piggery, and Kensington Gardens were dug up to plant cabbages – during which war?

2. Which flying machines attacked London with bombs in 1915?

3. Which fierce Celtic queen attacked Roman London and burned it to the ground?

4. Who were the first invaders of London after the Romans left?

5. Hendon is the home of a museum dedicated to which of the armed forces: the Royal Navy, the Army, or the Royal Air Force?

6. Which name, beginning with the letter 'b', was given to the bombing raids on London during the Second World War?

7. Which Prime Minister stayed in London throughout most of the Second World War?

8. Which nation attacked London with squadrons of bomber aircraft during the Second World War?

9. What was the name of the mercenary soldier who was employed to set light to the 36 barrels of gunpowder in the Gunpowder Plot of 1605?

10. In which year was Roman London burned to the ground: 61 AD, 79 AD, 204 AD, or 375 AD?

11. William 'Braveheart' Wallace was executed and had his head placed on a spike on London Bridge. Which country had he led in an uprising?

12. In the Peasants' Revolt, mobs of people from which two of the following English counties invaded London: Kent, Surrey, Yorkshire and Essex?

13. How many eggs per week was a Londoner allowed in 1942 under food rationing?

14. London Bridge was burned down in 1014 by King Ethelred to divide which attacking forces: the Vikings, the Normans or the Danes?

15. How many people were living in London at the start of the Second World War: 3 million, 6 million, 9 million or 12 million?

16. Which museum contains a Polaris nuclear missile and has two giant artillery guns outside it?

17. Where did over 170,000 Londoners shelter from bombs during the Blitz?

18. When was the last time London was invaded and occupied by forces from another country: 1066, 1432, 1644 or 1915?

19. In 1605, a plot to kill King James I involved placing barrels of gunpowder under which London building?

20. Who or what were known as 'blimps' during the Second World War: air raid wardens, anti-aircraft balloons, or sandbags?

21. To conserve fuel supplies, how many inches of heated bath water was a Londoner allowed during the Second World War?

22. In which year did the English Civil War begin, with fighting on the outskirts of London: 1638, 1641, 1642 or 1645?

23. Which Second World War cruiser is now a floating museum on the Thames?

24. A large Roman fort was built on which site: Cripplegate, Aldgate, Cheapside or Newgate?

25. What was the name, beginning with the letter 'c', of the forces loyal to King Charles I who fought during the English Civil War of 1642-6?

26. How many ships did the Danes sail up the River Thames with to attack London in 851 AD: 50, 150, 200 or 350?

27. How many Londoners were killed on the first night of the Blitz: 30, 130, 430 or 930?

28. According to legend, the British monarchy will never fall while which bird is living at the Tower of London?

29. Which one of the following was not a party to the Gunpowder Plot: Robert Catesby, John Browning, Thomas Winter or Francis Tresham?

30. How many tonnes of bombs were dropped on England during the First World War: 2.5 tonnes, 4 tonnes, 24 tonnes or 254 tonnes?

31. The Peasants' Revolt occurred under the reign of which king: Richard II, Henry VI or Edward II?

32. During the Blitz, the Plessey factory was moved underground - into which London Underground line?

33. Which item did it become compulsory for all Londoners to carry during the Second World War?

34. The uniform worn by Admiral Nelson when he was killed in battle is on display in a London museum. Which one?

35. How many hours a week were London air raid wardens required to work during the Second World War: 24, 48 or 72?

36. Between September 1940 and May 1941, how many Londoners were made homeless by bombing: 100,000, 240,000, 500,000 or 1,400,000?

37. During the Boer War, Dutch soldiers captured the Tower of London and the Stock Exchange: true or false?

38. What was the name, beginning with 'r', of the forces who fought the army of King Charles I during the English Civil War?

39. During Second World War rationing, a Londoner was allowed four ounces (a little over 100 grams) of ham - per day, per week or per month?

40. During the Gordon Riots of 1780, which three of the following prisons were burned down by angry mobs who released the prisoners: Fleet, Pentonville, Clerkenwell and Newgate?

41. What happened to 827,000 London schoolchildren in the early years of the Second World War?

42. An explosion at Clerkenwell in 1867 killed 12 and injured 126. Was this the work of Scottish nationalists, Prussian agents, Irish nationalists or an unknown group?

43. The Battle of Barnet occurred in 1471 - during the Wars of the Roses, the Hundred Years War or the Seven Years War?

44. During the Second World War, 2,340 German V1 flying bombs hit London. What was the nickname given to these weapons?

45. Did Alfred the Great, King Canute or Edward the Confessor oust the Danes and capture London in 886?

46. During Second World War rationing, a Londoner was allowed two ounces (55 grams) of cheese - per day, per week or per month?

47. In November 1642, royalist forces defeated parliamentary forces in a battle in which part of London: Brentford, Ealing, Islington or Earl's Court?

48. Where was the statue of Eros kept to protect it from damage during the Second World War: Egham, Hampton Court, Ealing or Guildford?

49. The moat around the Tower of London was used for growing vegetables during the Second World War: true or false?

50. During which war was Sir Roger Casement found guilty of planning an uprising, imprisoned in the Tower of London and then executed at Pentonville Prison?

# London landmarks (1)

1. The London Eye has 22, 32 or 42 capsules?

2. What is the name of the largest square in central London?

3. In which 'circus' would you find the statue of Eros sitting in a fountain?

4. Which Docklands building is the tallest in Britain?

5. Which museum's exterior is covered in carvings of animals?

6. Which famous London building has been a zoo, a mint and a jail during its history?

7. What is the name of the largest private home in London?

8. Which famous London sporting venue, currently being rebuilt, was opened in 1923?

9. Can you name either of the items held in the hands of the statue of Justice outside the Old Bailey?

10. Which 'circus' is located where Shaftesbury Avenue, the Haymarket and Regent Street all meet?

11. Which building, connected with astronomy, did Sir Christopher Wren build in Greenwich in 1675?

12. A statue of which famous black-and-white-movie actor stands in Leicester Square?

13. What is Big Ben: a clock, a tower housing a clock, or the bell inside a clock?

14. Which tall structure was completed in 1677 and requires visitors to walk up 311 steps to reach the top?

15. What shape is the church of Notre Dame de Paris (just off Leicester Square)?

16. How many people are buried under the floors of Westminster Abbey: 300, 1,000, 2,000, or over 3,000?

17. Which River Thames crossing opened in 1967?

18. What is the name of the Boy Scout building directly opposite the Natural History Museum?

19. The Crystal Palace was moved to Sydenham Hill from which central London park?

20. A revolving restaurant was opened in London in 1966 - on top of which building?

21. How much does the bell inside the famous clock tower of the Houses of Parliament weigh: 3 tonnes, 6 tonnes, 10 tonnes or 14 tonnes?

22. In which park would you find the Serpentine?

23. The Cabaret Mechanical Theatre contains many mechanical figures and scenes, called automata. Is this museum in Covent Garden, Oxford Circus or Regent's Park?

24. From which metal is the statue of Eros made: bronze, copper, aluminium or steel?

25. Which London park contains a boating lake, a peace pagoda and the British Genius Site?

26. Into which sea does the River Thames flow?

27. In which park would you find the Italian Fountains, completed in 1861?

28. How many huge statues of lions stand in Trafalgar Square?

29. Would you take a train to Manchester from Waterloo, Euston or Paddington station?

30. The Prospect of Whitby is one of London's oldest surviving public houses. In which century was it built?

31. London's first classical music museum was opened in 2001. What is it called?

32. Which country gave Cleopatra's Needle to Britain in 1819?

33. When was it erected on the Victoria Embankment: 1827, 1857, 1877 or 1897?

34. What was the name of Sir Francis Drake's flagship, a reconstruction of which is moored on the Thames in London?

35. What was the name of London's main fish market until 1982?

36. Which royal park forms the largest open space in central London?

37. Which palace is the London home of the Archbishop of Canterbury?

38. What object is Eros holding in the famous statue?

39. A ship which sailed from London to China in a record 107 days in 1871 is moored at Greenwich. What is its name?

40. Which London landmark is 520 m wide and has four main gates each weighing 3,700 tonnes?

41. How long does a trip on the London Eye take: 30 minutes, 45 minutes, 60 minutes or 75 minutes?

42. In which square would you find a statue of Sir Winston Churchill?

43. Which tall building on the South Bank of the River Thames used to be called Stamford Wharf, and now features the name of a well-known stock cube?

44. Which structure was built as an entrance to Buckingham Palace but was never used for that purpose?

45. Which tower, built in 1966, was London's tallest building until 1981?

46. Which famous abbey was first consecrated on 28 December 1065?

47. What is the maximum number of people each capsule of the London Eye can hold: 8, 16, 25 or 40?

48. How many masts, or struts, hold the Millennium Dome in place?

49. Who was the architect of the new Lloyd's Building which opened in London in 1986?

50. What is the name of the tower which houses Big Ben?

# Strange London

1. The hospital for the insane at Bedlam was a major tourist attraction in the 17th century: true or false?

2. According to London legend, which ancient warrior queen is buried beneath Platform 10 at King's Cross Station?

3. According to an old law, is it illegal to wear a top hat, beat a carpet or feed the ducks in a London royal park?

4. The crown jewels of which country are said to be buried somewhere in the region of Trafalgar Square?

5. Something you would expect to see in a building is missing from the Bank of England in central London. What is it?

6. In the 16th century, wealthy Londoners went to Bridewell Palace to watch a punishment being administered to vagrants and prostitutes. What was it?

7.  Which lady is not allowed to enter the City of London without the permission of the Lord Mayor?

8.  The City of London Police are reigning Olympic champions at which discontinued event?

9.  In 1674, a 'women's petition' against which type of drink was established in London?

10. How many people had dinner on top of Nelson's Column in 1842, just before the statue of Lord Nelson was put in place: 2, 4, 6 or 14?

11. During the Second World War, the baths in Buckingham Palace were marked with a black line to indicate the level of hot water (five inches) allowed by the Government: true or false?

12. What was introduced to Euston, Piccadilly and St James's Park stations in March 2001, but withdrawn the next day as it made people feel sick?

13. What is the name given to the corner of Hyde Park famous for people giving speeches and lectures on a variety of topics?

14. How long does it take for a waxwork in Madame Tussaud's to be made?

15. In February every year, a ceremony at the Roman Catholic church of St Etheldreda commemorates St Blaise. Is he the patron saint of those who suffer from sore throats, those who suffer from sore feet, or those who suffer from sore backs?

16. On which day of the week were theatres in 16th century London banned from performing because it was the traditional day for bear baiting?

17. Which one of the following can not be found in the 19th century time capsule underneath Cleopatra's Needle: a railway guide, a set of British coins, a book of Shakespeare, or 12 portraits of pretty English ladies?

18. The Science Museum is haunted by the ghost of a small child crushed under a steam engine in the 1890s: true or false?

19. The royal printers were fined £3,000 by King Charles I for a misprint in 1,000 copies of the Holy Bible. Did the misprint read 'Thou shalt commit adultery', 'Thou shalt steal', or 'Jesus was the son of Dog'?

20. James Hetherington was arrested on the Strand in 1797 - for wearing a top hat, nothing at all, or an Irish flag as a cloak?

21. Together with the King or Queen of England, the Vintners' and Dyers' Companies own all the birds of a certain species found on the Thames. Which bird is it?

22. Madame Tussaud made death masks of famous French aristocrats who were executed during the French Revolution: true or false?

23. It is illegal to impersonate a Chelsea Pensioner. What is technically still the heaviest punishment allowable by law for this crime?

24. Which South American animal is used for giving carriage rides round London Zoo?

25. In 1252, the Sheriffs of London were ordered to pay for the upkeep of a polar bear given to England as a gift from the king of which country?

26. The North Vietnam leader President Ho Chi Minh worked in London in 1913. Was he a lawyer, a senior military officer, or an apprentice pastry chef?

27. Was Roman Baths Road the site of the first Roman baths, the first heated swimming pool, or the first Turkish baths in London?

28. In the 1830s, King George IV licensed a London public house as a pawnbroker's after he had lost all his money. Did he lose it in a casino, at a horse race, at a cockfight, or at a greyhound race?

29. Which London pub is also a pawnbroker's today: the Castle, the Lamb, or the Cheshire Cheese?

30. Which pantomime character was based on a man who was Lord Mayor of London three times in the 15th century?

31. What sort of race would you see at Lincoln's Inn Fields on Shrove Tuesday?

32. Excavations at which London airport revealed the skeletons of wild hippos and elephants which once lived in the London area?

33. Why was the Palace of Westminster sited on the banks of the River Thames: so that it could receive wine and hams from boats on the river, so that its residents could go fishing, or so that it could not be completely surrounded by angry mobs?

34. Which financial institution was created by 150 brokers, fired from the Royal Exchange in the 1760s for rowdiness and misconduct?

35. Which London landmark was sold to an Arizona millionaire in 1971 and is now located in the United States?

36. Matthew Henderson murdered his mistress Lady Dalrymple in an argument. Was she angry because Henderson was seeing another woman, because he had stolen money from her, or because he had stepped on her toe?

37. In Victorian times, all hackney carriages in London had to be tall enough to accommodate a gentleman wearing a top hat: true or false?

38. At the Clink Prison, which prisoners were punished on a ducking stool: bakers who sold underweight bread, women who had affairs, or child thieves?

39. Joseph Swan was imprisoned in 1811 for receiving stolen goods. Were they the crown jewels, the skins of royal swans, or the printing plates of Dickens' *A Christmas Carol*?

40. Which bridge, only a few metres wide, had shops and houses built on it?

41. London's only commercial heliport is owned by which London store: Harrods, Selfridges, Harvey Nichols, or Liberty?

42. In 1721, a London production of which 'unlucky' Shakespeare play had to be broken up by the Army after the actors started attacking hecklers with swords?

43. Women convicted of petty treason under the 1351 Treason Act were given a terrible sentence. Were they burned at the stake, buried alive, or drowned in the Thames?

44. Why was the London district of Soho so named: because 'Soho' was a hunting call, because it was a type of beer, or because it was an abbreviation of 'Soldier's Hollow'?

45. An underground train ran between Paddington and Whitechapel for 70 years. What did it carry?

46. At the beginning of the 20th century, how much manure was produced each day by the horses used to pull London's trams and buses: 10 tonnes, 100 tonnes, 1,000 tonnes or 10,000 tonnes?

47. Between 1699 and 1706, convicted shoplifters were often branded – but on which part of their bodies?

48. In 2003, posters advertising a well-known shampoo appeared in London. They featured buttons which sprayed out a perfume when pressed. Were they found on bus shelters, at railway stations, or in chemists' shops?

49. According to an old law which has never been repealed, what should every London taxi carry at all times?

50. Motorists are allowed to drive on the right-hand side of the short road leading up to which London hotel?

# Made in London

1. Which famous fictional character lived at 221b Baker Street?

2. Name the London road which gave its name to a Beatles album and appeared in the photograph on its cover.

3. Kenwood House in Hampstead was used as a setting in which one of these films: *Spiderman*, *Shakespeare in Love*, or *Notting Hill*?

4. In the film *The World is Not Enough*, James Bond falls from a hot-air balloon on to the roof of which huge, temporary building in Greenwich?

5. Mary Poppins rose into the sky In front of the clock tower of which famous London building ?

6. Which London market is featured on the cover of the Oasis album *What's the Story, Morning Glory*?

7.  Which one of these films did not use London's Borough Market as a location: *Lock, Stock and Two Smoking Barrels*, *The X-Men*, or *The French Lieutenant's Woman*?

8.  Which famous London novelist visited his father in a London prison at the age of 12, and used the experience in his novels of London life?

9.  *A Man For All Seasons*, a film about Henry VIII and Sir Thomas More, was shot on location at which historic royal home?

10. The film *My Fair Lady* tells the tale of a flower seller who is transformed into a society lady - but which central London location was used as the setting for the market?

11. The owner of which famous London department store acted as a doorman at his own store in the comedy film *Mad Cows*?

12. Which 2001 action film featured scenes in the British Museum and on Tower Bridge, and a chase sequence involving old-fashioned double-decker London buses?

13. Who wrote the novel *London Fields*?

14. Which James Bond film featured a memorable high-speed boat chase down the River Thames from Westminster to Greenwich?

15. Who painted eighteen pictures of the River Thames in one month in 1899, all from the balcony of his room in the Savoy Hotel?

16. The novelist Daniel Defoe wrote *Moll Flanders* while he was in prison. Which prison was he in: Newgate, Clink or Fleet?

17. Australia House on the Strand was used in the Harry Potter films as the location for which fictional bank?

18. Which 1960s film, set in London, featured Michael Caine as a man with numerous girlfriends?

19. Which crime writer was the creator of Miss Marple and lived for a while in London's Sheffield Terrace?

20. The author of *The Owl and the Pussycat* and other nonsense verse was Master of Drawings for Queen Victoria, and produced scientific illustrations of birds for the Zoological Society of London. Who was he?

21. Which explorer's great literary work *The History of the World* was written in 1614 while the author underwent a lengthy imprisonment in the Tower of London?

22. Geoffrey Chaucer, author of the *Canterbury Tales*, worked on the River Thames. Was he a customs officer, a ferryman or a soldier?

23. Which London film studios are associated with a range of comedy films from the 1940s and the 1950s?

24. Lincoln's Inn Fields Theatre staged a production of *The Magician* in 1721. It was the first example of which type of show, popular with families?

25. In the film *Mission Impossible*, Tom Cruise's character hides out in offices above which London Underground station: Liverpool Street, Euston Square, or Westminster?

26. Which novelist wore ragged clothes and lived in rough accommodation in the East End's West India Docks and Limehouse in the 1920s?

27. Nick Hornby's novel *Fever Pitch* is about a supporter of which London football club?

28. Chatham Docks provided the setting for which river in the 1999 film *The Mummy*?

29. A building in Charing Cross Road was the setting for, and gave its name to, a bookshop in a novel (and a film). What was the novel called?

30. Ian Fleming named a Bond villain after the London architect (also his friend) who designed the Trellick Tower in Kensington and the building that is now the Sanderson Hotel. What was the villain's name?

31. In the Harry Potter films, which famous London attraction was used as the setting for Little Whinging Zoo?

32. Which famous author had a workmate called Bob Fagin when he worked in a factory as a boy?

33. Which author's ophthalmic practice in Devonshire Place was so quiet that he was able to write several of his Sherlock Holmes stories there?

34. The disused Beckton Gasworks was used as a setting for battle scenes in which Vietnam film: *The Deer Hunter*, *Full Metal Jacket*, or *Hamburger Hill*?

35. In which novel did George Orwell write about his experiences in the East End: *Animal Farm*, *Keep the Aspidistra Flying*, or *Down and Out in Paris and London*?

36. Peter Ackroyd's novel *Hawksmoor* is about the architect who helped to rebuild London after which of these disasters: the Blitz, the Black Death, or the Great Fire of London?

37. Seat 7 in the British Library's Reading Room was occupied every day for many months as the Communist manifesto *Das Kapital* was written - but by whom?

38. In the film *American Werewolf in London*, where does the werewolf wake in a cage after his rampages of the night before?

39. The sound of a famous London clock bell interrupts Cruella de Vil's therapy and causes it to fail in the Disney film *101 Dalmatians*. What is the name of the bell?

40. St Ermine's Hotel in Westminster had its ballroom transformed to look like the Savoy Hotel's dining rooms - but for which film: *Wilde*, *The Picture of Dorian Gray*, or *The Importance of Being Earnest*?

41. What did staff of the publisher John Murray do to the original manuscript of Lord Byron's memoirs when it arrived at their London offices in 1848?

42. The final scenes of *Bridget Jones' Diary* were shot outside a London Underground station. Was it Piccadilly Circus, Oxford Circus, Earl's Court or Holborn?

43. Sutton Square, Heston in west London was the location for key scenes in a film about an Asian girl who loves playing football. What is the name of the film?

44. Scenes in the Gwyneth Paltrow film *Possession* were shot inside which famous London museum during opening hours?

45. Which one of these films was not completely or partially filmed at Pinewood Studios: *Dr No*, *Tomb Raider II*, *Vertigo*, or *Thunderbirds*?

46. Which platform at King's Cross station was used as the mythical Platform $9\frac{3}{4}$ in the Harry Potter films?

47. In 1808, Richard Trevithick demonstrated his 'catch-me-who-can' device on the site where Euston Station now stands. What was the device?

48. The author of *Robinson Crusoe* was released from a London prison in the 17th century. In return, he acted as a spy for the British Government. Was he Daniel Defoe, William Wordsworth or Samuel Johnson?

49. Which London 'village' was the home of DH Lawrence and Robert Louis Stevenson, and is the current home of spy book author John le Carré?

50. Old Hall in Lincoln's Inn was the setting for the opening chapter of which Charles Dickens book: *David Copperfield, Great Expectations,* or *Bleak House?*

# Victorian & Edwardian London

1. Which monarch succeeded Queen Victoria?

2. Which London palace was called 'the people's palace' when it was completed in 1873: Alexandra Palace, Crystal Palace or Lambeth Palace?

3. How many horses were employed to pull London's buses and trams in 1900?

4. What opened between Deptford and London Bridge in 1836?

5. Which famous bookshop, whose name begins with the letter 'f', started trading in London in 1903?

6. In a meeting held in Tottenham Court Road in 1903, the Russian Social Democrat Party split into two groups. Which eventual leader of Russia was present at the meeting?

7. Seven London cemeteries opened in the 19th century. Which was the first: Brompton, Highgate, or Kensal Green?

8. Which theatre, designed to show Gilbert and Sullivan operas, was opened in 1881?

9. 'Pea souper' was a Victorian nickname for a weather and pollution condition which blighted London in the 19th century. What was it?

10. What was the population of Greater London at the time of Queen Victoria's death in 1901: 4.5 million, 5 million, 5.5 million or 6.5 million?

11. Which famous retailer opened a store in Oxford Street in 1909 after retiring from Marshall Field's of Chicago?

12. Which London park contains 19th century models of dinosaurs?

13. Which tunnel under the Thames was London's first, completed in 1843?

14. St Peter's Italian church was built in 1863. Was it the first Italian church to be built from concrete, to be built using steam-powered cranes, or to be built outside Italy?

15. What was placed on the corner of Fleet Street and Farringdon Street? Was it London's first telephone box, post box, parking meter or electric street light?

16. Which emergency service was founded in 1866 as a result of the Tooley Street Fire?

17. How many arches can be found in Admiralty Arch, a structure commissioned by King Edward VII?

18. Large-scale electric street lighting was fitted for the first time in London in 1878 – but along which riverside street?

19. How many passengers per day did London's horse-drawn buses and trams carry in 1900: 0.5 million, 1 million, 1.5 million, 2 million or 3 million?

20. What is the name of the Notting Hill market which was a popular street market from the 1870s onwards, but today has a reputation for antiques and collectables?

21. Taxis driven by the internal combustion engine appeared in London during the reign of which monarch: Queen Victoria, King Edward VII, or after the deaths of both?

22. During the Victorian era, Elizabeth Garrett Anderson qualified in London. Was she Britain's first woman doctor, lawyer, dentist or Member of Parliament?

23. In which year of King Edward VII's reign was the National Union of Journalists founded?

24. Which 1851 event was held in Hyde Park and featured 100,000 exhibits?

25. Which London market was the first to be lit by electric light: Brixton, Petticoat Lane, Camden, or Brick Lane?

26. How many horses per day were required to pull a horse bus in Victorian London?

27. In 1868, the first ever example of an item of street furniture was erected outside the Houses of Parliament. What was it?

28. Which department store was opened in Oxford Street in 1909?

29. Which political party was founded at the Congregational Memorial Hall in Farringdon Street in 1900?

30. Which industry employed the most Londoners for much of the Victorian era?

31. Free vaccinations against which disease were introduced in 1840 after an epidemic had killed 6,400 Londoners?

32. Which system of tunnels, proposed by Sir Joseph Bazalgette and still in use today, was introduced after the 'Great Stink' of 1858?

33. Which member of the Royal Family was a keen enthusiast of fire fighting and had his own uniform hanging up at Chandos Street Fire Station near Charing Cross?

34. The London-built steamship *The Great Eastern* was the largest ship in the world when it was launched in 1857. Which famous Victorian engineer designed it?

35. Thomas Carlisle founded which centre of learning in 1841: the London School of Economics, the London Library, or London University?

36. What happened to the River Thames in February 1855, causing London's docks to close and leading to the loss of 50,000 jobs?

37. Which street in a poor area of London was the centre of the second-hand clothes trade in Victorian times?

38. In 1881, how many people (on average) lived in each home in the Holborn area of London: 6, 8, 10 or 12?

39. What was the name given to the dense Victorian slums where criminals and gangs were said to live: Covens, Rookeries, Gangster Holes, or Vagabond Halls?

40. In 1842, what did *The Times* refer to as 'lumbering, clumsy conveyances in which the public are packed like coal sacks'?

41. In which year did work start on the construction of London's first underground railway: 1839, 1849 or 1859?

42. What was the London Underground's first nickname: the Time Tunnel, the Drain, the Great Conveyance, or the Underworld?

43. What was the average life expectancy in the poorest west London slum in the 1840s: 20 years, 16 years or 12 years?

44. What were goat-shay, gully, cherry-bobs and kiss-in-the-ring?

45. Which series of murders caused panic in London in 1888?

46. Which famous revolutionary political thinker lived in relative poverty in London after coming to England in 1849?

47. Which still-popular seasonal attraction was introduced in Roberts department store, Stratford in 1888?

48. How many free water fountains did the Metropolitan Free Drinking Fountain Association provide in London in the1870s: 30, 100, 300 or 1,000?

49. In Victorian London, what was a 'penny gaff'?

50. Were carriages, trains or pedestrians the sole users of the Rotherhithe Tunnel from 1843 to the1860s?

# London attractions

1. In which museum would you find the complete skeleton of a woolly mammoth?

2. Which attraction on Tooley Street features torture chambers and an exhibit of 'wicked women'?

3. The giant Teddy Bears' Picnic in Battersea Park is held on the first Friday of which month?

4. Where in London would you be able to view over 350 species of sea life including sharks?

5. Which London building houses, amongst other treasures, the Magna Carta, some original Beatles lyrics and Leonardo da Vinci's notebook?

6. Which London museum occupies part of the site of the former Covent Garden Flower Market: the London Dungeons, the London at War Experience, or the London Transport Museum?

7. Blue plaques mark London buildings in which famous people have lived. How many are on display today: 200, 500, 750 or 900?

8. Which famous Knightsbridge store started out in 1834 as a grocery and tea merchant's in Stepney, East London?

9. How many natural history specimens does the Natural History Museum hold: 3.5 million, 11 million, 23 million or 68 million?

10. What is the name of the most gruesome part of the Madame Tussaud's waxworks exhibition?

11. Which famous nurse has a museum in St Thomas' hospital dedicated to her life?

12. Which one of the following creatures can not be found at Plashet Zoo near East Ham: the chipmunk, the llama, the vulture or the wallaby?

13. The Museum of Childhood is in Bethnal Green. Is this in Islington, Hackney or Tower Hamlets?

14. In which month is the Great River Race between Richmond and Greenwich?

15. The Royal Horticultural Society organises the world's most famous flower show. What is it called?

16. Where in west London is the London Butterfly House: Bushey Park, Syon Park or Richmond Park?

17. The London Planetarium is located next to which other famous attraction on Marylebone Road?

18. Which famous writer, whose novels depicted London life, lived in a building in Doughty Street, now a museum?

19. Which museum houses the skeleton of Napoleon's horse: the National Army Museum, the Natural History Museum, the Museum of London, or the Imperial War Museum?

20. Which 14-storey London building receives 16,000 visitors a day, and houses over eight million stamps?

21. In which month of the year is the Hampton Court Flower Show held?

22. Housed in disused railway arches, Vinopolis is a centre for what sort of food or drink?

23. What is the name of the Piccadilly attraction which features waxworks and performing models of some of the world's most famous pop stars?

24. Which of the following museums offer free admission: the Science Museum, Pollock's Toy Museum, the National Maritime Museum, and the Clink Prison Museum?

25. Which museum recently added a Wellcome Wing and a 450-seat IMAX cinema?

26. How old is the oldest toy in Pollock's Toy Museum in central London: 500 years, 1,000 years, 3,000 years or 4,000 years?

27. Which of the following museums offer free admission: the Victoria & Albert Museum, the Design Museum, the British Museum, and the London Fire Brigade Museum?

28. The Daily Mail Ideal Home Show is held at which large exhibition centre?

29. In which month of the year is the Royal Windsor Horse Show held?

30. The Baishaki Mela is a festival celebrating the New Year. Is it Bengali, Punjabi or Thai?

31. The Petrie Museum is in Malet Place (near Goodge Street tube station). Is it dedicated to the history of medicine, Egyptian archaeology, housing in London, or cars and motorbikes?

32. Which important gardening event is held in May in the grounds of the Royal Hospital, Chelsea?

33. On 10 June every year, a gun salute marks the birthday of a member of the Royal Family. Which one?

34. Which famous regatta takes place in early July, on a stretch of the Thames a short distance west of London?

35. The Classic Car Run takes place at the beginning of November. The vintage vehicles travel, or try to travel, from London to which English town?

36. What is the name of the parade through the City of London which is held on the second Saturday of November every year?

37. Which South Kensington museum houses a large collection of dresses from 1600 to the present day, and galleries of Chinese, Japanese and Indian art?

38. On which day every year does the giant Christmas tree in Trafalgar Square have its lights switched on for the first time?

39. On which festive day in winter will you find swimmers competing in the Peter Pan Cup swimming race?

40. In which London pond or lake does this race take place?

41. In which London museum can you see Stephenson's Rocket and the Puffing Billy, the world's oldest surviving steam engine?

42. How many decorated floats are on parade in the Lord Mayor's Show: 40, 80, 100 or 140?

43. Which museum houses more than 1,000 historic timepieces and the Apollo 10 command module?

44. The Baishaki Mela is held In the streets around a famous lane in the East End. Which lane is it?

45. How long is the silence which is observed in London every Armistice Day?

46. At which cricket ground would you find the MCC Museum and the original Ashes?

47. Which museum features the Launch Pad - a series of 50 hands-on activities - in its basement?

48. Next to which canal is the London Canal Museum sited?

49. Which show is held at Earl's Court in early January: the International Motor Show, the International Boat Show, or the Ideal Home Show?

50. Which one of the following is not an exhibit in the Horniman Museum: a stuffed dodo, a Spanish Inquisition torture chair, the first steam engine, or voodoo dolls?

# Modern London

1. Which magician was suspended above London in a see-through box for 44 days in 2003?

2. On which side of the escalator is it considered polite to stand in London Underground stations?

3. Who became the first Mayor of London under a new system of local government in 2000?

4. In which London square did thousands of people assemble for New Year's Eve celebrations (before this was banned for safety reasons)?

5. A memorial fountain consisting of a stone oval 210 metres in diameter was built to honour a deceased member of the Royal Family. Who was she?

6. In which year was the congestion charge introduced in London?

7. Which institution moved from Bloomsbury to St Pancras in 1997-8?

8. Into which London station will the high-speed Channel Tunnel rail link travel?

9. Which famous auction house is located at 34-35 New Bond Street?

10. In which year did the poll tax riots break out in the Trafalgar Square area?

11. What is the name of the central London street in which the Treasury and most other government departments can be found?

12. If you were walking past the Almeida Theatre in Upper Street, would you be in Holborn, Islington, Paddington or St John's Wood?

13. In which park can you find the London Central Mosque?

14. Approximately how many black cabs are there in London: 1,400, 3,200, 19,000 or 36,000?

15. Which London-based institution receives a copy of every publication produced in the UK and Ireland?

16. London's most famous food store is at 181 Piccadilly. What is it called?

17. Which road, at right-angles to Oxford Street, is lined with shops selling computers and other electronic equipment?

18. Would you find Berwick Street fruit and vegetable market in Soho, the East End or Notting Hill?

19. If you were in Lillywhites in Lower Regent Street, would you be buying DVDs, suits, books or sports equipment?

20. Which was the most popular London attraction of 1999: the British Museum, the London Eye, or Westminster Abbey?

21. Which political office does the resident of Number 11 Downing Street usually hold?

22. From which country do the most tourists come to visit London?

23. Who lived at Number 10 Downing Street before Tony Blair moved in: John Major, Margaret Thatcher or James Callaghan?

24. How many people actually live in the City of London: 4,000, 6,000 or 10,000?

25. London is divided into Greater London boroughs. How many are there: 13, 23 or 33?

26. Which Greater London borough extends the furthest north: Islington, Barnet or Enfield?

27. A new bridge across the Thames experienced 'wobbling problems' at the beginning of the 21st century. What is it called?

28. Which ex-boxer was arrested for demonstrating outside Number 10 Downing Street in 2003?

29. In which year did London celebrate Queen Elizabeth II's Golden Jubilee?

30. On average, how many passengers used the Docklands Light Railway every day in July 2003: 95,000, 155,000, 175,000 or 215,000?

31. Where is London's biggest Caribbean market regularly held: Brixton, Notting Hill, Spitalfields, or Brick Lane?

32. In 2003, a blue plaque was put up to commemorate the author of the classic horror novel *Frankenstein*. Who was she?

33. Pubs near a certain London market are allowed to serve alcohol with breakfast from 7a.m. to fit in with the working hours of market porters. Which is the market?

34. In which year did London black cabs have to start providing wheelchair access?

35. Which sports team paraded through London and was met by the Prime Minister after its dramatic success in November 2003?

36. Which of the following countries sends the most tourists to London: Germany, Italy, Sweden or the Netherlands?

37. Which country sends a Christmas tree to London every year (it stands in Trafalgar Square)?

38. How many MPs represent London constituencies in Parliament: 26, 38, 56 or 74?

39. How much was the daily congestion charge payable by London's motorists in 2003?

40. What is the name of the Russian billionaire who became the owner of a London football club in 2003?

41. In which year did Londoners vote for the Greater London Assembly and the Mayor in a referendum?

42. Which of these Greater London boroughs is the furthest east: Havering, Bexley or Barking?

43. London contains the largest permanent public building built in the UK in the 20th century. Is it the Royal Festival Hall, the British Library or the National Film Theatre?

44. How many people visited the Millennium Dome in the year that it was open: 1.5 million, 3.5 million, 4.5 million or 6.5 million?

45. How many species of fish live in the River Thames: fewer than 30, between 30 and 60, between 60 and 100, or more than 110?

46. Princess Michael of Kent opened a new museum on 8 May 2003. Is the museum dedicated to pop music, fashion, tea and coffee, or dolls?

47. What happened to the admission charges at many London museums in 2001? Were they raised, lowered or dropped?

48. Which Greater London borough extends furthest south: Bromley, Croydon or Lewisham?

49. Foyles is one of many bookshops on the road which links Tottenham Court Road to Cambridge Circus. What is the name of the road?

50. In which year did the form of public transport called the Riverbus start operating on the Thames: 1948, 1963 or 1989?

# London's famous people

1. Which London architect reshaped large areas of central London after the Great Fire of 1666?

2. Who led the Iceni tribe in a revolt against the Romans which included an attack on Londinium?

3. Which famous film director was born in Leytonstone High Road and directed films including *Rear Window* and *Vertigo*?

4. In which street, known for its medical connections, was the nurse Florence Nightingale born?

5. Who established a 'ragged school' for poor children in Stepney in 1867 (the first of many acts related to child welfare in London)?

6. Did Wat Tyler lead the Peasants' Revolt, the Gordon Riots or the Cato Street Conspiracy in London?

7. Which 'fab four' shared a flat at 57 Green Street (near Hyde Park) in 1963?

8. Jonas Hanway of London was the first person to use a certain device for keeping off the rain (in 1750). What was the device?

9. Which female writer was a founder member of the Bloomsbury Group, so named after the part of London in which its members met?

10. Name the famous naturalist who was born in Marlborough Street in 1809.

11. Charles Dickens hoped to be buried locally when he died in Kent, but in which London building was he finally laid to rest?

12. Which famous psychiatrist and psychoanalyst lived and died at 20 Maresfield Gardens, Hampstead?

13. Who broadcast radio signals from the top of the General Post Office at Aldersgate in 1896?

14. Penicillin was discovered by Alexander Fleming - while he was working at which London hospital: Paddington, St Mary's, or St Bartholomew's?

15. What is the name of the lead singer of the band Blur, who was born in Leyton?

16. By what name is William Pratt, born in Forest Hill Road, better known: Boris Karloff, Bill Wyman or Eddie Izzard?

17. Which round-the-world explorer discovered California and claimed it for Queen Elizabeth I?

18. There is a statue of Sir Henry Irving in St Martin's Place. It is the only statue commemorating someone of his profession in central London. What was he?

19. Which successful England football manager was born in Dagenham?

20. Londoner Sir Giles Gilbert-Scott designed Battersea Power Station – as well as which item of London street furniture, famous since the 1930s?

21. In 1926, John Logie Baird demonstrated a certain device in a room above what is now Bar Italia in Soho. What was it?

22. Spencer Perceval is the only person to have been shot and killed in which famous London building?

23. In which cemetery would you find the tomb of Karl Marx?

24. Which artist, best known for his limericks and nonsense verse, was born in London in 1812?

25. Which American writer, whose real name was Samuel Langhorne Clemens, lived in Tedworth Square, London in the 1890s?

26. Which famous American comedian was born in the London suburb of Eltham in 1903: Bob Hope, Bill Cosby or Eddie Murphy?

27. Born in London's East End, Jack Cohen named his group of stores after his wife Tess. Which supermarket chain arose as a result?

28. Which fashion designer founded the Fashion and Textile Museum in Bermondsey Street?

29. The American inventor of Morse Code lived in London between 1812 and 1815. What was his name?

30. Which very famous Austrian composer wrote his first symphony in London in 1764?

31. A blue plaque at 20 Barons Court Road marks the visit of which famous Indian statesman (when he was a law student)?

32. Who made his conducting debut with the Clapton Music Society before going on to conduct the Proms concerts for half a century?

33. Which Dutch artist, whose sunflowers and self-portraits are world-famous, worked in Lambeth as a trainee art dealer in the 19th century?

34. A flamboyant pop singer put about £800,000 worth of clothes and other items from his Holland Park home on sale at Sotheby's in September 2003. Who is he?

35. In 1890, which one of these men used his entire wealth (£40) to open a tiny shop at 55a Fleet Street, where he sold hand-rolled cigarettes to journalists: Louis Rothman, Peter Stuyvesant or Phillip Marlborough?

36. Londoner Samuel Pepys is famous for his diaries of 17th century London. He was imprisoned in the Tower of London because it was believed that he was selling military secrets to the French: true or false?

37. Which famous literary Londoner coined the saying 'When you are tired of London, you are tired of life'?

38. In which area of London do Bryan Adams, Eric Clapton and Bob Geldof all have homes: Chelsea, Islington or Hampstead?

39. An all-British aircraft made its first flight over Walthamstow Marshes in 1909. Who designed it: AV Roe, Thomas Sopwith or Harold Hawker?

40. David Ben-Gurion lived in Warrington Crescent in Maida Vale - before becoming the first prime minister of which new country?

41. In which part of south London was the supermodel Naomi Campbell born: Balham, Streatham or Tooting?

42. The first prime minister of a newly independent India lived some 30 years earlier in Elgin Crescent, London W11. What was his name?

43. In the 1670s, Aphra Behn became the first woman in London to take up a certain profession. Did she work as a judge, earn a living from writing, or conduct an orchestra?

44. Londoner Sir Ronald Ross was awarded a Nobel Prize in 1902 - for his work on understanding which contagious disease?

45. The originator of the penny post system lived in the Royal Free Hospital, Hampstead from 1849 to 1879. Who was he?

46. Which pop singer splashed out £2.5 million on a Chelsea Harbour home in 2003, making Michael Caine one of his neighbours?

47. Heavyweight boxing champion Lennox Lewis was born in London – in Leytonstone, Putney, West Ham or Dulwich?

48. Which Italian 'ladies' man' had an eventful nine-month stay in London in 1763 when he courted five sisters and endured a short spell in Newgate Prison?

49. In the Second World War, what was the name of the high-ranking German officer who became the last-ever prisoner to be held in the Tower of London?

50. Peter the Great, the Tsar of Russia, worked in London in the late 17th century. Was he a lawyer, an apprentice shipbuilder, or a diplomat?

# Fun & games in London

1. The home stadium of English Rugby Union lies to the south-west of central London. What is its name?

2. What is the nickname of Arsenal Football Club?

3. If you were eating strawberries and cream next to Centre Court, which sport would you be watching?

4. Which sports event is London bidding to host in 2012?

5. Which London football club did the owner of Harrods buy in the late 1990s?

6. Which county cricket club plays its matches at Lord's in north London?

7. Which long-distance running event, sponsored by Flora from 1996 to 2006, has its starting points at Blackheath Common and Greenwich Park?

8. Which London football club is nicknamed 'the Hammers'?

9. Which London bridge is the starting point for the annual Oxford and Cambridge Boat Race?

10. Which famous sporting event is held at the All England Club in south-west London?

11. How many racetracks (for horses) are there in London?

12. Which football club moved from south London to Milton Keynes in 2003?

13. Which county cricket club plays its matches at the Oval in south London?

14. Which sport takes place at Catford Stadium and Walthamstow Stadium: motorcycle racing, greyhound racing, or athletics?

15. Which London football team is named after a wartime munitions factory?

16. If you were jogging through London's oldest royal park, would you be in Greenwich Park, Hyde Park or Regent's Park?

17. In which busy London street would you find Hamleys, the world-famous toyshop?

18. Which London football team's home ground is called Griffin Park?

19. In which year did London first host the Olympic Games?

20. What is the name of London's only professional Rugby League club?

21. In which year was the London Marathon first run?

22. For which of London's home counties did cricketer Phil Tufnell play?

23. Which London football club has its home ground on the Isle of Dogs in south-east London: Millwall, Leyton Orient, or Brentford?

24. Eight London football clubs took part in a new competition in 1871. What competition was it?

25. Which of these cruel sports was hugely popular in London during the reign of Queen Elizabeth I: bear baiting, foxhunting, or cat fighting?

26. Which cricket ground hosted the first FA Cup Final?

27. Which London sporting landmark used to be considered the home of football, and is currently being redeveloped?

28. Is the Harlequins' home ground at Welford Road, the Stoop, or Hackney Field?

29. What sort of children's show was first put on at Covent Garden in 1662?

30. What is the name of the south London sports centre which is also Britain's national sports centre?

31. Which London royal park features a running track?

32. Herne Hill Velodrome is a cycling circuit. Is it the smallest, the oldest or the most costly one in the world?

33. What kind of sports facility is available to the public in the courtyard of Somerset House for two months of the year: an ice rink, a show jumping arena, or a swimming pool?

34. Which London football team's home ground is known as 'the Valley'?

35. Funland is London's largest video game centre. How many video games are available there: over 50, over 150, over 250 or over 400?

36. Name one of the two London teams which play in the British Basketball League.

37. In which year (after the Second World War) did London host the Olympic Games?

38. What is the name of the tennis club in Hammersmith which hosts a warm-up event before Wimbledon?

39. Which London football team counts Phil Collins and Emma Bunton among its fans?

40. What was the name of the London ice hockey team which played at the London Arena in Docklands until 2003?

41. Which England batsman and wicket keeper, who also played county cricket for Surrey, retired in 2003?

42. The indoor game of real tennis was first played on courts at which historic royal residence?

43. Against which European team did England play its last football match at Wembley Stadium in 2000?

44. A playground in Kensington Gardens features a model of a pirate ship. Which member of the Royal Family does it commemorate?

45. Which football club plays at Loftus Road in London's Shepherd's Bush?

46. Is Legoland in Windsor, Barnet, Croydon or Docklands?

47. The NAMCO station, a large indoor entertainment centre featuring dodgem cars and ten-pin bowling, is housed inside a former local government building. Which one?

48. Where has the London Marathon finished every year since 1993: the Strand, the Embankment, the Mall, or Trafalgar Square?

49. Which famous rock singer once owned Watford Football Club?

50. In which park was London's last racetrack (for horses): Alexandra Park, Wimbledon Park, or Finsbury Park?

# London –
# glam & grunge

1. Which London-born musician created the personas of Aladdin Sane and Ziggy Stardust during the 1970s?

2. Which rock opera with a biblical theme opened in the West End in the early 1970s?

3. In which month of 1977 did Queen Elizabeth II's Silver Jubilee celebrations take place?

4. Which much-loved ska group hailed from north London and was fronted by a singer called Suggs?

5. In which year did the London Stock Exchange finally begin admitting women?

6. In 1976, the 100 Club in Oxford Street hosted the first festival of a new kind of popular music. What was it?

7. What was sold in litres for the first time in London in 1981?

8.  At which venue did the 1985 Live Aid concert take place?

9.  In 1986, a fire started by a bedside candle devastated parts of a royal building to the west of London. Which building was it?

10. The 1988 FA Cup Final ended in a shock win for which south London team over the favourite, Liverpool?

11. Which company opened its first UK outlet in Woolwich, south-east London, in 1974?

12. Which London Underground station was the scene of a devastating fire in 1987?

13. Which aircraft began regular passenger services from London's Heathrow Airport in 1976?

14. In the 1978 Oxford and Cambridge Boat Race, which crew sank more than 1.5 km before the finishing line?

15. Which device was introduced in 1983 to counter illegal parking?

16. Whose wedding dress featured 10,000 pearls and pearl sequins, and an 8-metre train?

17. Which darts player won his first world championship in 1980 and was nicknamed the Crafty Cockney?

18. In which building did Princess Anne's wedding to Captain Mark Phillips take place in 1973?

19. Which film archive and cinema complex was built near Waterloo Bridge in the 1970s?

20. Which musician's drawings were removed from a London gallery by the Obscene Publications Squad during the 1970s?

21. In the 1980s, Michael Fagan caused an uproar by breaking into a London building. Which building was it?

22. In 1973, Britain's first commercial radio station went on air from a London studio. What was the name of the station?

23. Which punk group sailed a boat up the Thames to the Houses of Parliament in a publicity stunt in 1977?

24. In 1983, there was a major robbery from a Brinks Mat warehouse at Heathrow Airport. What was the value of the gold ingots that were stolen?

25. Who moved into Number 10 Downing Street in 1979?

26. Which London team won the English League / FA Cup double in 1971?

27. Who won the women's singles tennis title at Wimbledon in 1977, the year of the Queen's Silver Jubilee?

28. Where were the offices of Stiff Records, the home of seventies and eighties music acts Elvis Costello, Madness, and the Damned: Camden Town, Wapping, Ealing or Finsbury Park?

29. Which much-loved London boxer won the European Heavyweight title in 1970?

30. In which year was it announced that the Greater London Council was to be abolished?

31. Which London punk band released an album called London's Calling?

32. A 1975 crash on the London Underground killed 42 people - at which station?

33. At which London museum did the Tutankhamen exhibition attract over two million visitors?

34. What was the name of the London venue in which alternative stand-up comedy developed in the early 1980s?

35. What was the name of the theatre which opened on London's South Bank in 1976?

36. Who was the last leader of the Greater London Council?

37. Which influential rock guitarist died in the Cumberland Hotel, Marylebone on 18 September 1970?

38. Which part of London was massively regenerated during the 1980s, including the building of Canary Wharf and Hays Galleria?

39. In which year did *Les Misérables* open in London?

40. Which member of the Royal Family won the 1971 BBC Sports Personality of the Year award?

41. In 1988 three trains collided, killing over 30 people - at which London station?

42. Who described an extension to London's National Gallery as a 'monstrous carbuncle'?

43. Which London arts centre opened in 1983?

44. Which London punk band released *The Great Rock 'n' Roll Swindle* in 1979?

45. Which Andrew Lloyd Webber musical, successful in the West End, was based on a TS Eliot poem?

46. For which London team did veteran defender Bobby Moore make his final appearance in an FA Cup match in 1975?

47. What was the name of the London fashion store, owned by Malcolm McLaren, in which several members of the Sex Pistols worked and met?

48. Which Andrew Lloyd Webber musical opened in London in 1989?

49. In October 2003, a life-sized bronze statue of a 1970s singer-songwriter was unveiled in south-west London - just metres from the spot where he died in a car crash. Who was he?

50. Carl André's controversial sculpture, a simple rectangle of bricks, went on show at which London gallery in 1976?

# Out & about in London

1. Name the world's longest-running play, which opened in London in 1952.

2. In which royal park was the *Picnic with Pavarotti* concert attended by over 70,000 people in 2001?

3. By which short nickname are the Promenade Concerts better known?

4. Which form of entertainment did Oliver Cromwell ban when he came to power in 1649: theatres, choirs, or art galleries?

5. In which central London square do tourists queue to buy half-price West End theatre tickets?

6. Which London art gallery was founded in 1824 with just 38 pictures, but now displays more than 50 times that number?

7. By which name was the Forum music venue previously known?

8. Which theatre was the first building in London to have electric lights?

9. Would you find the Mean Fiddler (a live music venue) in Harlesden, Camden or Brixton?

10. In which London cinema did Paul McCartney play a 2003 gig featuring many songs from the Beatles' back catalogue?

11. In which London park is there a famous open-air theatre in the summer months?

12. In which one of the following theatres were no Shakespeare plays ever performed: the Hope Theatre, the Rose Theatre, or the Globe Theatre?

13. Which historic rock and pop venue, once located in Wardour Street, was reopened in Islington in 2002?

14. Which children's hospital in Bloomsbury receives all the royalties from sales of the book *Peter Pan*?

15. The King's Head, the Hen and Chickens and the Old Red Lion are Islington pubs. Apart from eating and drinking, what can you do in all three pubs?

16. Which former Australian soap star has a £1.5 million home in London's Kensington?

17. During the reign of Elizabeth I, a number of theatres sprang up next to the River Thames. On which bank?

18. Where is the Tricycle Theatre: Harlesden, Southwark, Kilburn or Holborn?

19. Which London museum is the biggest in the UK?

20. In which art gallery would you find Van Gogh's most famous self-portrait: the Courtauld Institute Gallery, the National Portrait Museum, or the Hayward Gallery?

21. What was used in a London theatre for the first time in 1881?

22. In which London park is the Fleadh Irish music festival held?

23. Which mythical beast gives its name to a children's theatre - the oldest children's theatre in London?

24. What is the name of the theatre beside the Thames which is an exact replica of the building in which Shakespeare's plays were performed 400 years ago?

25. Are the Meccano Club, the Red Rose and Headliners: modern art galleries, comedy clubs, or music venues?

26. Which Covent Garden building is the home of the Royal Ballet?

27. Which American singer owns a £1 million London home with her husband Guy Ritchie?

28. At which London arts centre is the London Symphony Orchestra based?

29. Which musician played his first UK gig at the music venue Water Rats near King's Cross station: Elvis Presley, Bob Dylan, or Bruce Springsteen?

30. The London Film Festival is held in various locations in Soho and the West End. Has the festival been running for more than 20 years, more than 45 years, or more than 70 years?

31. Which London theatre is famous for a ghost called 'the man in grey', whose skeleton was found in the walls during the 1840s: the Theatre Royal (Drury Lane), the Strand Theatre, or the Aldwych Theatre?

32. Which London art gallery contains over 7,000 images of famous Britons?

33. Which of these would you go to see or hear at the Wigmore Hall: ballet, rock music, classical music, or dance?

34. The Courtauld Institute is famous for its collection of Old Masters and is located in an 18th century building. Is it County Hall, Somerset House, or Mansion House?

35. Which West End theatre has hosted the highly successful musical *Chicago* for many years?

36. Which was the only London theatre not to close during the Second World War: the Windmill Theatre, the Savoy Theatre, the Duke of York Theatre, or the Westminster Theatre?

37. At which modern art gallery is the winner of the Turner Prize announced every year: Tate Britain, Tate Modern, or the Saatchi Gallery?

38. Which of these would you go to see or hear at Sadlers Wells in Islington: dance, comedy, jazz music, or Shakespearean theatre?

39. If you were listening to new bands at the Rock Garden, in which tourist area of London would you be?

40. Name the art gallery which opened in 1970 and stands near a London lake with which it shares its name.

41. The Spitalfields Music Festival is held in June - and which other month of the year?

42. Which is the oldest public picture gallery in England: the National Portrait Gallery, the Hayward Gallery, or the Dulwich College Picture Gallery?

43. The London Jazz Festival is usually held in November - but in which area of central London?

44. The Party in the Park is a large pop concert which takes place in Hyde Park. The proceeds go to a charity – which one?

45. Which of these is based at the Coliseum: the English National Opera, the London Philharmonic Orchestra, or the Royal Opera?

46. The Meltdown Festival is held every June – but in which hall on the South Bank?

47. The Phoenix Theatre on Charing Cross Road has been showing the same play for the last decade. Can you name it?

48. If you were listening to new bands at the Garage, would you be in Covent Garden, Islington or Shepherd's Bush?

49. Which arts centre is the London home of the Royal Shakespeare Company, and features three towers called Lauderdale, Shakespeare and Cromwell?

50. King Charles II allegedly first spied his mistress Nell Gwynn at a theatre which is now in London's West End. Which one?

# London people, London life

1. People considered to be true cockneys must have been born within earshot of the bells of which church?

2. How many extra temporary staff are drafted in for the Harrods Summer Sale: 100, 300, 1,000 or 3,000?

3. Many thousands of Huguenot refugees fled to London in the 17th and 18th centuries. From which country did they come?

4. What does the cockney rhyming slang 'apples and pears' stand for?

5. What was the population of Greater London according to the 2001 Census: just over 6 million, just over 7 million, or just over 8 million?

6. If you were in Bangla Town, known for its Bengali and Bangladeshi communities, would you be near Brick Lane, Lambeth Road or Euston Road?

7. Was London's first mosque built in Stepney, Wood Green, Willesden, or Tooting?

8. What is the name of London's main meat market?

9. Wembley and Harrow are home to London's largest community of which faith group: Buddhists, Sikhs or Hindus?

10. What is the telephone area code for inner London?

11. Wesley's Chapel on City Road is the mother church for which religion?

12. Has the Brick Lane Mosque previously been a Protestant church, a synagogue, or both?

13. There were approximately 1,000 black inhabitants of London in 1786. From which country had the majority fled?

14. Which city overtook London as the world's biggest city in 1957?

15. Approximately how many shoppers visit Harrods on the first day of its Summer Sale: 15,000, 25,000, 50,000, 100,000 or 250,000?

16. When did British banknotes first carry a picture of the king or queen's head: 1740, 1820, 1840 or 1960?

17. Which was the largest immigrant group in London in the Victorian era?

18. Which famous London tradition started among market traders in 1875?

19. What is the name of the Egyptian owner of the famous Harrods department store?

20. In which part of London did many German immigrants settle during the Victoria era?

21. How many floors does the famous London toyshop Hamleys occupy?

22. In what circumstances did the first Jews come to Britain: with William the Conqueror, at the invitation of Oliver Cromwell, or with the increase in the shipping trade in the 17th century?

23. Which language did the Norman invaders bring to London and use for government business?

24. Which is the largest Catholic church in London?

25. When were parking meters introduced in London: 1948, 1958 or 1968?

26. In 1811, London became the first city in the world to have a population greater than: 0.5 million, 1 million, 2 million or 3 million?

27. What does the cockney rhyming slang 'whistle and flute' mean?

28. Is Denmark Street (off Charing Cross Road) best known for its music shops, bookshops, antique shops, or clothes shops?

29. Why did so many Irish people came to London in the 1840s?

30. Which colourful feature of cockney London was founded by Henry Croft in 1875?

31. If you were talking about your 'saucepan lids' in cockney rhyming slang, to what would you be referring?

32. Tom Sawyer's funeral in Highgate attracted over 100,000 mourners. Was he a bare-knuckle fighter, a clown, an opera singer, or a highwayman?

33. Sailors of which nationality settled in Limehouse during the 1850s?

34. In which year did London Transport license buskers on its stations for the first time?

35. Until which decade of the 20th century was Covent Garden London's biggest fruit and vegetable market?

36. Russian and Polish Jews escaped persecution in their homelands by coming to London in the 19th century. Did the majority settle in Stepney, Holborn, Ealing or Battersea?

37. Which Regent Street shop opened in 1875 to sell fabrics from the East - with just a 16 year-old girl and a Japanese boy as staff: Liberty, H&M, Oasis, or John Lewis?

38. Asian refugees fled to London in the early 1970s to escape persecution by their country's leader Idi Amin. From which African nation did they come?

39. The Bevis Marks synagogue near Petticoat Lane is the oldest synagogue in Britain. How old was it in 2001: 100, 200, 300 or 500?

40. 492 immigrant workers arrived in London on board the *Empire Windrush* in 1948 - from which Caribbean island?

41. The East London Mosque Trust founded a mosque in 1941. Was it the first, second or third mosque to be built in the city?

42. At which London market is a turkey auction held every Christmas Eve?

43. In which year did the London Central Mosque open in Regent's Park: 1955, 1966, 1977 or 1988?

44. Is 'One never knows' the motto of the Methodist Church, the Pearly Kings and Queens, or London's Jewish community?

45. Columbia Road Market in Bethnal Green is held every Sunday. Does it sell books, old and retro clothing, plants and flowers, or second-hand cars?

46. The first Sikh Temple in London, a Gurdwara, was built in 1902. Was this in Turnham Green, Barons Court, Shepherd's Bush or Battersea?

47. Of which community is Green Lanes in north London the centre: Italian, Cypriot or Spanish?

48. Approximately how many people of Chinese origin live in London: 10,000, 30,000, 60,000 or 90,000?

49. What does the cockney rhyming slang 'Lady' (short for 'Lady Godiva') stand for?

50. Which area of London was known in the past for its large number of Brazilian people, earning it the nickname Brazilwater?

# London landmarks (2)

1. Was Tower Bridge completed in the 17th, 18th, 19th or 20th century?

2. The Church of St Martin-in-the-Fields overlooks which famous London square?

3. The White Tower is part of which historic London building?

4. Which London building consists of over 1,100 rooms connected by more than 3 km of passageways?

5. West of London lies a castle which is the oldest royal home in Britain. What is it called?

6. Which royal building in the centre of London has 78 bathrooms and its own post office?

7. The Royal Hospital, Chelsea is a retirement home for old soldiers. What are they known as?

8. There is a statue of Richard I (Richard the Lionheart) in Old Palace Yard. Does it portray him at prayer, as a foot soldier, or mounted on a horse?

9. Can you name one of the bridges on either side of the Millennium Bridge?

10. Is the reconstructed Globe Theatre on the north or the south side of the River Thames?

11. Which of these London parks is the furthest west: Hyde Park, Holland Park or Green Park?

12. If you were riding a horse along Rotten Row, in which royal park would you be?

13. Which column was built to commemorate the Great Fire of London and stands near London Bridge?

14. Which of these bridges over the Thames is the furthest east: Battersea Bridge, Vauxhall Bridge or Putney Bridge?

15. Was Hammersmith Bridge, which opened in 1827, London's first metal bridge, first suspension bridge or first concrete bridge?

16. The tiered design of St Bride's Church in Fleet Street is believed to have inspired which feature of wedding receptions?

17. Marble Arch contains a small office. Was it a public house, a police station, or a secret meeting place for the aristocracy?

18. King Henry III spent over $\frac{1}{10}$ of his entire wealth rebuilding which London building?

19. Why was Canary Wharf so named - because it handled banana boats from the Canary Islands, because it handled ships full of tropical birds from the Caribbean, or because it was founded by Joseph Canary in 1763?

20. Which London church has the second-biggest dome (after St Peter's in Rome)?

21. Bankside Power Station now houses which modern art gallery?

22. Which London bridge links the South Bank with Charing Cross?

23. One of London's bridges was built during the Second World War, largely through the efforts of female workers. Was it Waterloo Bridge, Hammersmith Bridge or Hungerford Bridge?

24. Which London bridge features a deck that splits in two, rising to allow tall ships to pass through?

25. Which London church is a brass-rubbing centre: St Paul's, Southwark Cathedral, St Martin-in-the-Fields, or St Bride's?

26. Which name was given to the huge glass building which held the 1851 Great Exhibition?

27. Windsor Castle was built by Henry VIII: true or false?

28. After which member of the Royal Family is the bridge over the River Thames at Dartford named?

29. Which London church has a 'Whispering Gallery'?

30. Which measurement is marked by the Greenwich Meridian at the Royal Observatory?

31. Which very tall London structure, built from Scottish granite, commemorates a British military commander?

32. The Millennium Dome is big enough to house the Statue of Liberty: true or false?

33. Which famous architect was responsible for St Paul's Cathedral?

34. What is the name of the Shakespearean theatre which burned down in 1613 and has recently been rebuilt?

35. In which year did the Thames Barrier have its official opening: 1984, 1988, 1992 or 1996?

36. Which famous museum, opened in 1881, houses zoological and fossil collections?

37. Constitution Arch at Hyde Park Corner features a giant bronze statue showing the Goddess of Peace. How many Horses of War is she taming?

38. Which central London road is home to the jewellery trade, especially the diamond business?

39. The Millennium Dome is big enough to house the Empire State Building: true or false?

40. A large circular building stands on Chalk Farm Road. It was originally a steam engine turning shed and was more recently a theatre, cinema and arts centre. What is it called?

41. Which east London river is the largest tributary of the Thames?

42. A statue believed to date from 1395 stands in Trinity Street. Who does it show?

43. Which London theatre faces Temple Station across the River Thames?

44. If you were admiring the plants in the Palm House, where would you be?

45. How many floors has London's tallest building, Canary Wharf: 40, 50, 60 or 70?

46. What is the name of the north London area in which the Grand Union Canal joins the Regent's Canal?

47. Which tower, a tribute to Queen Victoria, stands in the grounds of Imperial College?

48. What colour is the statue of a small boy which marks the spot where the Great Fire of London was halted in 1666?

49. Which Greek god is depicted in a huge bronze statue in Hyde Park?

50. Which futuristic-looking building, designed by Richard Rogers, houses a famous insurance company?

# London ancient & modern

1. Who proclaimed 'Veni, vidi, vici' after making a successful raid on south-east England in 54 BC?

2. What does 'Veni, vidi, vici' mean?

3. Which Roman temple, dating back almost two millennia, was discovered in London after the Second World War: the Temple of Apollo, the Temple of Diana, or the Temple of Mithras?

4. Which Roman road ran along the route which is now Holborn, Oxford Street and Bayswater Road: Watling Street, Fosse Way, or Silchester Road?

5. Which area of central London, famous for its literary connections, was originally used as a breeding ground for pigs?

6. In the Domesday Book, was the value placed on Peckham 30 shillings, £30, £300 or £3,000?

7. What was the capital city of England before London?

8. What is the saintly name of London's oldest hospital?

9. In 1348-9, which disease wiped out almost $\frac{1}{3}$ of London's population?

10. Which private school, originally part of a monastery, was opened by Queen Elizabeth I in 1560?

11. King John used to go hunting in what is now a south London borough. He was so pleased with his sport that he granted the area the right to hold an annual fair. What is the name of the borough?

12. At the end of the Civil War in 1653, which famous London figure was appointed Lord Protector?

13. Was London's first coffee house founded in the 15th, 16th, 17th or 18th century?

14. In 1650, stage wagons started regular services between London and Liverpool. How many days did this trip take in summer?

15. And how many days in winter?

16. What was the name of the London-based egalitarian political group founded during the Civil War: the Cavaliers, the Levellers, or the New Model Army?

17. Was Harrow School founded in 1420, 1495, 1572 or 1603?

18. How many Londoners per week were being killed by the Great Plague when it was at its peak in 1665: 3,000, 5,000, 8,000 or 14,000?

19. The largest commercial dock in the western world was built in London in 1693. Was it called Howland Great Wet Dock, London Dock, or Elizabeth Dock?

20. Which financial institution was set up in 1694 and has the nickname 'the Old Lady of Threadneedle Street'?

21. In 1700, approximately what percentage of England's imports was being handled in London's docks: 30%, 50%, 60%, 80% or 100%?

22. The first British police force was formed In 1798. Was it the Marine Police Force, the City of London Police Force, or the Royal Parks Police?

23. The southern part of Hampstead Heath was called Hatch's Bottom. Until 1777, was it a swamp, a leper colony, or both?

24. Which newspaper printed its first issue in 1788: *The Evening Standard*, *The Times*, or *The Daily Telegraph*?

25. Was Rotherhithe's Greenland Dock used by pirates, whalers, Atlantic traders, or the Royal Navy?

26. Which area of London derives its name from Fulke's Hall and was still a village in the 18th century?

27. How many days did it take to travel from London to Edinburgh by coach in the mid-18th century?

28. What was the name of Britain's first art school, founded in 1768, which still exists as a major gallery today?

29. By the end of the 18th century, $\frac{1}{3}$ of all the leather produced in Britain was processed in London – in Bermondsey, Putney or Hammersmith?

30. In 1733, the Fleet was covered and built over. Was the Fleet a market square, a river or a giant mural?

31. Which gentlemen's club was formed by Sir Walter Scott, Humphrey Davy and Michael Faraday in 1824: the Athenaeum, the Royal Automobile Club, or the Londoners' Club?

32. Which of these was established in 1829: London's first regular newspaper, London's first horse-drawn bus service, or London's first postal service?

33. An outbreak of a certain disease resulted in the deaths of more than 6,000 Londoners in 1831-2. Was it flu, cholera or malaria?

34. Bon Marché, Britain's first department store, opened in 1877. Was it in Oxford Street, Brixton, Kensington or Hampstead?

35. Where was Queen Victoria buried when she died in 1901: Buckingham Palace, Westminster Abbey, St Paul's, or Highgate Cemetery?

36. What was briefly banned from London's streets in 1906 for being too noisy?

37. What was the date of the end of the First World War, marked by a crowd of 100,000 outside London's Mansion House?

38. 65,000 people were employed at the most important site of the London arms industry during the First World War. What was it called?

39. How many Londoners were killed in combat during the First World War?

40. London's first Woolworths store opened in 1924. Was it in Oxford Street, Regent Street, Ealing Broadway or Hammersmith Avenue?

41. In which year did the General Strike almost cause London to grind to a halt?

42. Which BBC service was set up in 1932, broadcasting around the globe from Bush House in the Strand?

43. How many London houses were destroyed during the Second World War: 94,000, 116,000 or 142,000?

44. What was the name of the steel bomb shelter issued free to 2 million families during the Second World War?

45. A group of criminals planned a notorious 1960s robbery in the Ship and Blue Ball public house near Liverpool Street station. By what name is the robbery known?

46. Which county ceased to exist in 1965 when, together with parts of other counties, it was formed into a new area called Greater London?

47. In which year, after the Second World War, did the Festival of Britain take place?

48. In 1991, the dog show Crufts moved out of London to another British city. Which one?

49. Which famous British screen and stage actress became MP for Hampstead in 1992?

50. Which record-breaking aircraft made its final landing at Heathrow Airport on 24 October 2003?

# London for experts

1. A plaque on which famous London church marks the exact centre of London?

2. Which two tube stations have the word 'black' in their names?

3. Which one of the following was not a Millennium Dome 'zone': the Living Island Zone, the Money Zone, the Faith Zone, the Charity Zone, the Self-Portrait Zone, or the Journey Zone?

4. Which ruler of Britain had been dead for 18 months when his body was dug up, hanged and then beheaded?

5. Name the first statue in London to be made from aluminium.

6. Today, people who visit shops without intending to buy anything are called 'window shoppers'. What were they called in early 20th-century London: tabbies, scroungers or valaguards?

7.  What, in London, travels an average 1.2 million km in its 'lifetime'?

8.  The famous actor Sir Henry Irving managed London's Lyceum Theatre. Irving's business manager was also the author of *Dracula*. Who was he?

9.  Which historic document recognised the right of Londoners to elect a mayor?

10. Simon FitzMary, a former Sheriff of London, opened an institution in 1247. Was it a university, an asylum, a science laboratory, or a prison?

11. What was the name of Green Park tube station until 1937?

12. The Fingerprint Branch of the Metropolitan Police opened in 1900 - with how many staff?

13. The Vanguard Omnibus Company is thought to be the first coach company to operate double-decker buses from London to a certain seaside town – in 1904. Which town was this?

14. The air in the London Underground system is hotter, on average, than the air above ground level. How many degrees hotter?

15. What was the nickname given to England's first asylum for the insane, founded at Bishopsgate?

16. Which of these was the statue in Piccadilly Circus known as Eros built to represent: charity, hope, love or dignity?

17. At the request of Queen Victoria, one London police station was not designated by a blue lamp - because these reminded her of the 'blue room' in which her husband died. Can you name the police station?

18. Which London Underground line has 127 of the network's 400+ lifts?

19. Name the king who used force to try to control London, but ended up being killed when he was run through with a red-hot poker.

20. Dr Crippen's arrest for murder was based on an early example of which police technique: taking fingerprints, using the telegraph, or working from identikits?

21. Which bus service has the longest daytime route, travelling a distance of 32.6 km between Ilford and Harold Wood: the 116, the 6, or the 296?

22. Who was the last monarch to wash the feet of the poor during the Maundy Thursday ceremony?

23. A river used to flow from south Hampstead into the Thames. What was its name?

24. In which year was the first tunnel under the Thames opened: 1842, 1886 or 1904?

25. Jill Viner was the first woman to perform which job in London in 1974?

26. To which part of London did Charles Dickens' family move when he was 10 years old, providing him with inspiration for the Micawbers' house in *David Copperfield* and the Cratchits' house in *A Christmas Carol*?

27. Which structure, on the Embankment, is the oldest outdoor artefact in London?

28. Which US president was married in the London church All-Hallows-by-the-Tower: Benjamin Franklin, George Washington, John Quincy Adams, or Abraham Lincoln?

29. The second tunnel to be excavated under the River Thames took fewer years to complete than the first. How many years fewer?

30. The Rose Theatre was the first bankside playhouse of the Elizabethan era, opening in 1587. With whose plays was it particularly associated?

31. Which column was built in 1834, allegedly funded by the 'voluntary' donation of one day's pay by every man in the British Army?

32. Which was the smallest church in the City of London, built in 1390 but destroyed by an IRA bomb in 1993?

33. By 1896, the founder of a certain children's charity had appeared in court 88 times for abducting children to save them from child abuse. Which charity was it?

34. Which renowned American inventor and statesman worked as a printer at the London church St Bartholomew the Great?

35. Which Act of Parliament saw an end to the famous London 'pea-souper' smogs in 1956?

36. The nursery rhyme London Bridge is Falling Down comes from a Norse poem - from which century?

37. Where did Billingsgate fish market move to in 1982?

38. A conspiracy to assassinate the Cabinet was uncovered in 1820. By what name is it known?

39. Which area did Charles Dickens describe as 'the filthiest, the strangest, the most extraordinary of the many localities that are hidden in London'?

40. Which famous Victorian housing trust, founded by an American banker, was set up in 1862?

41. Which Victorian Londoner is often credited with being the first to recommend (in 1837) the building of underground railways: William Hogarth, the Earl of Shaftesbury, or Charles Pearson?

42. Who was London's most successful and prolific builder of the 19th century?

43. In 1851, how many people visited the Great Exhibition of the Works of Industry of All Nations?

44. Which London actor's real name is Maurice Micklewhite?

45. William Walworth stabbed Wat Tyler (the leader of the Peasants' Revolt) to death. What position of power did Walworth hold at the time?

46. What was the name of the tube station, opened in 1907 and closed in 1932, which was used as an underground bomb shelter by Winston Churchill until the Cabinet War Rooms in Whitehall were built?

47. The Priory of St Mary of Bethlehem was founded in London many centuries ago. By what name is it better known?

48. Lollards' Tower was used as a prison for religious dissenters. In which famous London palace can it be found?

49. Which Cadbury's chocolate bar is the biggest seller in tube station vending machines?

50. The Prince of Wales used to visit a certain London restaurant with the actress Lily Langtry. Their visits were so frequent that they had a special door constructed to ensure that they entered unobserved. Was the restaurant Rules, Claridge's, or the Savoy Grill?

# Answers

QUIZ 1 **London for beginners**

1. The Thames
2. The tube
3. Heathrow
4. Dark blue
5. Buckingham Palace
6. Westminster
7. Red
8. 5 November
9. True
10. Chelsea
11. Oxford Street
12. The Notting Hill Carnival
13. Black
14. The Lawn Tennis Championships at Wimbledon
15. Over 1,000 million
16. The pigeon
17. Red
18. Westminster
19. The Piccadilly Line
20. East
21. False
22. The West End
23. North
24. True
25. Marylebone Road
26. Pimlico
27. Queen Elizabeth II
28. The Northern Line
29. Cricket
30. 10
31. Black
32. Barons Court, Earl's Court, Ravenscourt Park and Tottenham Court Road
33. Madame Tussaud
34. Nelson's Column
35. Green
36. Piccadilly Circus
37. The Natural History Museum
38. Dorset
39. Hampton Court Palace
40. Football
41. Peter Pan
42. The Tower of London
43. Twice
44. The Romans
45. White City or Whitechapel
46. The 17th century
47. The Millennium Dome
48. Germany
49. The Changing of the Guard
50. False

QUIZ 2 **Royal London**

1. Queen Victoria
2. St Paul's Cathedral
3. Autumn
4. Westminster Abbey
5. The Tower of London
6. King George VI
7. June
8. King Richard I (Richard the Lionheart)
9. Seven
10. King George III
11. Queen Elizabeth the Queen Mother
12. The Trooping of the Colour
13. Kensington Palace
14. Windsor Castle
15. King Henry VIII

16. Buckingham Palace
17. St James's Palace
18. Horseguards Parade
19. £28,000
20. A bearskin
21. Beefeaters
22. The Festival of Remembrance
23. King Charles I
24. The Mall
25. Prince Albert
26. The Victoria & Albert Museum
27. The Queen is in residence
28. Kensington Palace
29. King Henry VIII
30. Westminster Abbey
31. 1993
32. Holland Park
33. King Henry VIII
34. The Cenotaph
35. Anne Boleyn and Lady Jane Grey
36. Buckingham Palace
37. Queen Victoria
38. Marlborough House
39. True
40. Purses of money
41. The House of Lords
42. Hyde Park
43. The Household Cavalry
44. The state carriages and horses
45. 1066
46. The Royal Botanic Gardens, Kew
47. The Houses of Parliament
48. The Ceremony of the Keys
49. Wash the feet of the poor
50. 1837

### QUIZ 3  Olde London

1. The Romans
2. Wimbledon Common
3. William Caxton
4. 6
5. The Bank of England
6. Whitehall Palace
7. Londinium
8. True
9. London Bridge
10. The Romans
11. The 18th century
12. The Great Plague
13. Sir Francis Drake
14. Saxon
15. The Strand
16. The beginning of the Great Fire of London
17. One
18. The Tudors
19. Judaism
20. A baker's
21. York
22. Highgate
23. On the River Thames when it froze over
24. 1123
25. 87
26. The Great Plague
27. True
28. King Canute
29. The Black Death
30. Lundenwic
31. A guild of craftsmen who made knife handles out of ivory
32. Pipe makers
33. Smithfield Market
34. About 50,000
35. True
36. Fleet Street
37. Edward II
38. 604
39. Cats and dogs
40. Snuff and tobacco

41. St Albans
42. Westminster
43. 400 years
44. One (1665 and 1666)
45. Rats

46. Sir Christopher Wren
47. Farringdon Street
48. Druids
49. The north side
50. The last Frost Fair

## QUIZ 4 London transport

1. The Piccadilly Line
2. 5 guineas
3. Waterloo
4. The Victoria Line
5. The M25
6. The first
7. The Waterloo & City Line
8. 5.4 million
9. Parking fines
10. The District Line (60 stations)
11. 118,000 km
12. The District Line
13. True
14. The East London Line and the Bakerloo Line
15. Greenford
16. London Gatwick
17. Covent Garden and Leicester Square
18. Victoria
19. London City Airport
20. The Jubilee Line
21. The Knowledge
22. Elephant and Castle
23. The M4
24. Bethnal Green

25. Waterloo
26. King's Cross and Charing Cross
27. Six
28. The Northern Line
29. Four
30. The Central Line
31. Steam
32. West
33. A commercial heliport
34. London Gatwick
35. St Paul's
36. Rotherhithe and Vauxhall
37. Docklands Light Railway
38. Park Lane
39. Heathrow
40. Warren Street
41. Nearly 19 hours
42. Vauxhall Cross
43. Hampstead
44. The Victoria Line
45. Chalk Farm
46. An escalator
47. East
48. Wimbledon Park
49. King's Cross St Pancras
50. Victoria Embankment

## QUIZ 5 London crime

1. The Metropolitan Police
2. New Scotland Yard
3. Five
4. True
5. An umbrella
6. Marble Arch

7. A horse thief
8. A public hanging
9. Jack the Ripper
10. More than 300
11. Ronnie and Reggie Kray
12. The Old Bailey

## Answers

13. Boiling them in oil
14. Brixton
15. Public executions
16. The Great Train Robbery
17. True
18. South London
19. The forerunners of the Metropolitan Police
20. Christine Keeler
21. Harrods
22. The Notting Hill Carnival
23. False
24. Dick Turpin
25. The blue lamp
26. 999
27. 56
28. Newgate
29. 100,000
30. The Tower of London

31. Ronnie Biggs
32. The East End
33. 24
34. 215
35. George Blake
36. Jack Fenshaw
37. Dr Crippen
38. 1973
39. The Metropolitan Police
40. $\frac{1}{4}$
41. Pentonville Prison
42. Ronan Point
43. Her half-sister
44. Fulham
45. 5p
46. Sir Robert Peel
47. Colonel Thomas Blood
48. Tottenham
49. Ruth Ellis
50. True

---

**QUIZ 6** **London's Swinging 60s**

1. Carnaby Street
2. Ronnie Scott's
3. Vidal Sassoon
4. The betting shop
5. The Marquee Club
6. Abbey Road
7. Kings Road
8. The Beatles
9. Aldermaston
10. A daisy
11. Hyde Park
12. The Small Faces
13. Biba
14. Anthony Newley
15. The kipper tie
16. David Bowie
17. The Chelsea boot
18. Parking tickets
19. The Kinks
20. Pickles
21. David Bailey
22. Soho
23. Ossie Clark

24. Michael Caine
25. Twiggy
26. True
27. Sandie Shaw
28. A post code was added
29. Simon and Garfunkel
30. Carnaby Street
31. The Beatles
32. Jimi Hendrix
33. Stamford Brook
34. Joe Orton
35. The Rolling Stones
36. The trolley bus
37. Smog
38. Eel Pie Island
39. 1969
40. Tommy Steele
41. The Marquee Club
42. Tottenham Hotspur
43. The Yardbirds
44. The Twist
45. The Greater London Council

46. Fulham
47. The Establishment

48. BBC2
49. MFI
50. The Victoria Line

## QUIZ 7 **London at war**

1. The Second World War
2. Zeppelin airships
3. Boudicca
4. The Saxons
5. The Royal Air Force
6. The Blitz
7. Sir Winston Churchill
8. Germany
9. Guy Fawkes
10. 61 AD
11. Scotland
12. Kent and Essex
13. One
14. The Danes
15. 9 million
16. The Imperial War Museum
17. In the London Underground
18. 1066
19. The Houses of Parliament (House of Lords)
20. Anti-aircraft balloons
21. Five
22. 1642
23. HMS Belfast
24. Cripplegate
25. Cavaliers

26. 350
27. 430
28. The raven
29. John Browning
30. 254 tonnes
31. Richard II
32. The Central Line
33. The gas mask
34. The National Maritime Museum
35. 72
36. 1,400,000
37. False
38. Roundheads
39. Per week
40. Fleet, Clerkenwell and Newgate
41. They were evacuated from London
42. Irish nationalists
43. The Wars of the Roses
44. Doodlebugs
45. Alfred the Great
46. Per week
47. Brentford
48. Egham
49. True
50. The First World War

## QUIZ 8 **London landmarks (1)**

1. 32
2. Trafalgar Square
3. Piccadilly Circus
4. Canary Wharf
5. The Natural History Museum
6. The Tower of London
7. Buckingham Palace
8. Wembley Stadium

9. A set of scales and a sword
10. Piccadilly Circus
11. The Royal Observatory
12. Charlie Chaplin
13. The bell inside a clock
14. The Monument
15. Circular
16. Over 3,000

## Answers

17. The Dartford Tunnel
18. Baden-Powell House
19. Hyde Park
20. The Telecom Tower
21. 14 tonnes
22. Hyde Park
23. Covent Garden
24. Aluminium
25. Battersea Park
26. The North Sea
27. Hyde Park
28. Four
29. Euston
30. The 16th century
31. The Handel House Museum
32. Egypt
33. 1877
34. The *Golden Hind*
35. Billingsgate
36. Hyde Park
37. Lambeth Palace
38. A bow
39. The *Cutty Sark*
40. The Thames Flood Barrier
41. 30 minutes
42. Parliament Square
43. The OXO Tower
44. Marble Arch
45. The Telecom Tower
46. Westminster Abbey
47. 25
48. 12
49. Richard Rogers
50. St Stephen's Tower

---

**QUIZ 9** **Strange London**

1. True
2. Boudicca
3. Beat a carpet
4. France
5. Windows
6. Flogging (whipping)
7. The Queen
8. The tug of war
9. Coffee
10. 14
11. True
12. Perfume to make the air smell better
13. Speakers' Corner
14. Six months
15. Those who suffer from sore throats
16. Thursday
17. A book of Shakespeare
18. False
19. 'Thou shalt commit adultery'
20. A top hat
21. The swan
22. True
23. Death
24. The llama
25. Norway
26. An apprentice pastry chef
27. The first Turkish baths
28. At a cockfight
29. The Castle
30. Dick Whittington
31. A pancake race
32. Heathrow
33. So that it could not be completely surrounded by angry mobs
34. The Stock Exchange
35. London Bridge
36. Because he had stepped on her toe
37. True
38. Bakers who sold underweight bread
39. The skins of royal swans
40. Old London Bridge
41. Harrods
42. *Macbeth*

43. Burned at the stake
44. 'Soho' was a hunting call
45. Letters and parcels

46. 1,000 tonnes
47. Their faces
48. On bus shelters
49. A bale of hay
50. The Savoy

## QUIZ 10 Made in London

1. Sherlock Holmes
2. Abbey Road
3. *Notting Hill*
4. The Millennium Dome
5. The Houses of Parliament
6. Berwick Street Market
7. *The X-Men*
8. Charles Dickens
9. Hampton Court
10. Covent Garden
11. Harrods
12. *The Mummy Returns*
13. Martin Amis
14. *The World Is Not Enough*
15. Claude Monet
16. Newgate
17. Gringotts Bank
18. *Alfie*
19. Agatha Christie
20. Edward Lear
21. Sir Walter Raleigh
22. A customs officer
23. Ealing Studios
24. The pantomime
25. Liverpool Street
26. George Orwell
27. Arsenal

28. The Nile
29. *84 Charing Cross Road*
30. Goldfinger (the architect was called Erno Goldfinger)
31. London Zoo
32. Charles Dickens
33. Sir Arthur Conan Doyle
34. *Full Metal Jacket*
35. *Down and Out in Paris and London*
36. The Great Fire of London
37. Karl Marx
38. London Zoo
39. Big Ben
40. *The Importance of Being Earnest*
41. They burned them
42. Piccadilly Circus
43. *Bend It Like Beckham*
44. The British Museum
45. *Vertigo*
46. Platform 4
47. A steam train on a circular track
48. Daniel Defoe
49. Hampstead Village
50. *Bleak House*

## QUIZ 11 Victorian & Edwardian London

1. King Edward VII
2. Alexandra Palace
3. 50,000
4. London's first railway line
5. Foyles
6. Lenin
7. Kensal Green

8. The Savoy Theatre
9. Smog
10. 6.5 million
11. Gordon Selfridge
12. Crystal Palace
13. Rotherhithe Tunnel
14. To be built outside Italy

15. London's first post box
16. The Metropolitan Fire Brigade
17. Five
18. Embankment
19. 2 million
20. Portobello Market
21. King Edward VII
22. Doctor
23. 1907
24. The Great Exhibition
25. Brixton
26. 12
27. A set of traffic lights
28. Selfridges
29. The Labour Party
30. Clothing manufacture
31. Smallpox
32. The sewage system
33. King Edward VII
34. Isambard Kingdom Brunel
35. The London Library
36. It froze
37. Petticoat Lane
38. 10
39. Rookeries
40. Omnibuses
41. 1859
42. The Drain
43. 12 years (in the Potteries slum, west of Notting Hill)
44. Victorian children's street games
45. The Whitechapel Murders
46. Karl Marx
47. Santa's Christmas grotto
48. 300
49. A crude, improvised theatre
50. Pedestrians

## QUIZ 12 London attractions

1. The Natural History Museum
2. The London Dungeons
3. August
4. The London Aquarium
5. The British Library
6. The London Transport Museum
7. 750
8. Harrods
9. 68 million
10. The Chamber of Horrors
11. Florence Nightingale
12. The vulture
13. Tower Hamlets
14. September
15. The Chelsea Flower Show
16. Syon Park
17. Madame Tussaud's
18. Charles Dickens
19. The National Army Museum
20. The British Library
21. July
22. Wine
23. The Rock Circus
24. The Science Museum and the National Maritime Museum
25. The Science Museum
26. 4,000 years
27. The Victoria & Albert Museum and the British Museum
28. Earl's Court
29. May
30. Bengali
31. Egyptian archaeology
32. The Chelsea Flower Show
33. The Duke of Edinburgh
34. Henley Regatta
35. Brighton
36. The Lord Mayor's Show

37. The Victoria & Albert Museum
38. 1 December
39. Christmas Day
40. The Serpentine
41. The Science Museum
42. 140
43. The Science Museum
44. Brick Lane
45. Two minutes
46. Lord's
47. The Science Museum
48. Regent's Canal
49. The International Boat Show
50. The first steam engine

## QUIZ 13 **Modern London**

1. David Blaine
2. The right
3. Ken Livingstone
4. Trafalgar Square
5. Princess Diana
6. 2003
7. The British Library
8. St Pancras
9. Sotheby's
10. 1990
11. Whitehall
12. Islington
13. Regent's Park
14. 19,000
15. The British Library
16. Fortnum & Mason
17. Tottenham Court Road
18. Soho
19. Sports equipment
20. The British Museum
21. The Chancellor of the Exchequer
22. The United States
23. John Major
24. 6,000
25. 33
26. Enfield
27. The Millennium Bridge
28. Chris Eubank
29. 2002
30. 155,000
31. Brixton
32. Mary Shelley
33. Smithfield
34. 2000
35. The England Rugby Union team
36. Germany
37. Norway
38. 74
39. £5
40. Roman Abramovich
41. 1998
42. Havering
43. The British Library
44. 6.5 million
45. More than 110
46. Fashion
47. They were dropped
48. Croydon
49. Charing Cross Road
50. 1989

## QUIZ 14 **London's famous people**

1. Sir Christopher Wren
2. Boudicca
3. Alfred Hitchcock
4. Harley Street
5. Dr Thomas Barnardo
6. The Peasants' Revolt
7. The Beatles
8. An umbrella
9. Virginia Woolf
10. Charles Darwin
11. Westminster Abbey
12. Sigmund Freud

## Answers

13. Marconi
14. Paddington
15. Damon Albarn
16. Boris Karloff
17. Sir Francis Drake
18. An actor
19. Sir Alf Ramsey
20. The red public telephone box
21. The television
22. The House of Commons (he was Prime Minister)
23. Highgate
24. Edward Lear
25. Mark Twain
26. Bob Hope
27. Tesco
28. Zandra Rhodes
29. Samuel Morse
30. Wolfgang Amadeus Mozart
31. Mahatma Gandhi
32. Sir Henry Wood
33. Vincent Van Gogh
34. Sir Elton John
35. Louis Rothman
36. True
37. Dr Samuel Johnson
38. Chelsea
39. AV Roe
40. Israel
41. Streatham
42. Jawaharlal Nehru
43. She earned a living from writing
44. Malaria
45. Sir Rowland Hill
46. Robbie Williams
47. West Ham
48. Casanova
49. Rudolf Hess
50. An apprentice shipbuilder

---

### QUIZ 15 Fun & games in London

1. Twickenham
2. The Gunners
3. Tennis
4. The Summer Olympic Games
5. Fulham
6. Middlesex
7. The London Marathon
8. West Ham
9. Putney Bridge
10. The Lawn Tennis Championships at Wimbledon
11. None
12. Wimbledon
13. Surrey
14. Greyhound racing
15. Arsenal
16. Greenwich Park
17. Regent Street
18. Brentford
19. 1908
20. The London Broncos
21. 1981
22. Middlesex
23. Millwall
24. The FA Cup
25. Bear baiting
26. The Oval
27. Wembley Stadium
28. The Stoop
29. A Punch and Judy show
30. Crystal Palace
31. Regent's Park
32. The oldest
33. An ice rink
34. Charlton Athletic
35. Over 250
36. The Towers or the Leopards
37. 1948
38. The Queen's Club
39. Tottenham Hotspur
40. The London Knights

41. Alec Stewart
42. Hampton Court Palace
43. Germany
44. Princess Diana
45. Queen's Park Rangers

46. Windsor
47. County Hall
48. The Mall
49. Sir Elton John
50. Alexandra Park

## QUIZ 16 London – glam & grunge

1. David Bowie
2. *Jesus Christ Superstar*
3. June
4. Madness
5. 1973
6. Punk
7. Petrol
8. Wembley Stadium
9. Hampton Court
10. Wimbledon
11. McDonald's
12. King's Cross
13. Concorde
14. Cambridge
15. The wheel clamp
16. Princess Diana
17. Eric Bristow
18. Westminster Abbey
19. The National Film Theatre
20. John Lennon
21. Buckingham Palace
22. The London Broadcasting Company (LBC)
23. The Sex Pistols
24. £26 million

25. Margaret Thatcher
26. Arsenal
27. Virginia Wade
28. Camden Town
29. Henry Cooper
30. 1985
31. The Clash
32. Moorgate
33. The British Museum
34. The Comedy Store
35. The National Theatre
36. Ken Livingstone
37. Jimi Hendrix
38. Docklands
39. 1986
40. Princess Anne
41. Clapham Junction
42. Prince Charles
43. The Barbican
44. The Sex Pistols
45. *Cats*
46. Fulham
47. Sex
48. *Aspects Of Love*
49. Marc Bolan
50. The Tate Gallery

## QUIZ 17 Out & about in London

1. *The Mousetrap*
2. Hyde Park
3. The Proms
4. Theatres
5. Leicester Square
6. The National Gallery
7. The Town and Country
8. The Savoy Theatre
9. Harlesden

10. Leicester Square Odeon
11. Regent's Park
12. The Hope Theatre
13. The Marquee Club
14. Great Ormond Street Hospital
15. See plays
16. Holly Valance
17. South

## Answers

18. Kilburn
19. The British Museum
20. The Courtauld Institute Gallery
21. Electric lighting
22. Finsbury Park
23. The unicorn
24. The Globe
25. Comedy clubs
26. The Royal Opera House
27. Madonna
28. The Barbican
29. Bob Dylan
30. More than 45 years
31. The Theatre Royal (Drury Lane)
32. The National Portrait Gallery
33. Classical music
34. Somerset House
35. The Adelphi Theatre
36. The Windmill Theatre
37. Tate Britain
38. Dance
39. Covent Garden
40. The Serpentine Gallery
41. December
42. Dulwich College Picture Gallery
43. Soho
44. The Prince's Trust
45. The English National Opera
46. The Royal Festival Hall
47. *Blood Brothers*
48. Islington
49. The Barbican Centre
50. The Theatre Royal (Drury Lane)

## QUIZ 18  London people, London life

1. Bow
2. 3,000
3. France
4. Stairs
5. Just over 7 million
6. Brick Lane
7. Stepney
8. Smithfield Market
9. Sikhs
10. 0207
11. Methodism
12. Both
13. The USA
14. Tokyo
15. 250,000
16. 1960
17. The Irish
18. Pearly Kings and Queens
19. Mohammed Al Fayed
20. Camden Town
21. Seven
22. With William the Conqueror
23. French
24. Westminster Abbey
25. 1948
26. 1 million
27. Suit
28. Music shops
29. To escape the Irish Famine
30. Pearly Kings and Queens
31. Your kids (children)
32. A bare-knuckle fighter
33. Chinese
34. 2003
35. The 1970s
36. Stepney
37. Liberty
38. Uganda
39. 300
40. Jamaica
41. The first
42. Smithfield
43. 1977
44. Pearly Kings and Queens
45. Plants and flowers
46. Shepherd's Bush

47. Cypriot
48. 60,000

49. A fiver (a £5 note)
50. Bayswater

## QUIZ 19 **London landmarks (2)**

1. The 19th century
2. Trafalgar Square
3. The Tower of London
4. The Houses of Parliament
5. Windsor Castle
6. Buckingham Palace
7. Chelsea Pensioners
8. Mounted on a horse
9. Southwark Bridge or Blackfriars Bridge
10. The south side
11. Holland Park
12. Hyde Park
13. The Monument
14. Vauxhall Bridge
15. First suspension bridge
16. The wedding cake
17. A police station
18. Westminster Abbey
19. Because it handled banana boats from the Canary Islands
20. St Paul's
21. The Tate Modern
22. Hungerford Bridge
23. Waterloo Bridge
24. Tower Bridge
25. St Martin-in-the-Fields
26. The Crystal Palace
27. False
28. Queen Elizabeth II
29. St Paul's
30. 0° longitude
31. Nelson's Column
32. True
33. Sir Christopher Wren
34. The Globe Theatre
35. 1984
36. The Natural History Museum
37. Four
38. Hatton Garden
39. False
40. The Round House
41. The River Lea
42. Alfred the Great
43. The National Theatre
44. The Royal Botanic Gardens, Kew
45. 50
46. Little Venice
47. Queen's Tower
48. Gold
49. Achilles
50. The Lloyd's Building

## QUIZ 20 **London ancient & modern**

1. Julius Caesar
2. 'I came, I saw, I conquered'
3. The Temple of Mithras
4. Silchester Road
5. Bloomsbury
6. 30 shillings
7. Winchester
8. St Bartholemew's
9. The Black Death
10. Westminster School
11. Peckham
12. Oliver Cromwell
13. The 16th century
14. 10 days
15. 12 days
16. The Levellers
17. 1572
18. 8,000
19. Howland Great Wet Dock

## Answers

20. The Bank of England
21. 80%
22. The Marine Police Force
23. A swamp
24. *The Times*
25. Whalers
26. Vauxhall
27. 14 days
28. The Royal Academy of Arts
29. Bermondsey
30. A river
31. The Athenaeum
32. London's first horse-drawn bus service
33. Cholera
34. Brixton
35. Buckingham Palace
36. The bus
37. 11 November 1918
38. The Woolwich Arsenal
39. 124,000
40. Oxford Street
41. 1926
42. BBC World Service
43. 116,000
44. The Anderson shelter
45. The Great Train Robbery
46. Middlesex
47. 1951
48. Birmingham
49. Glenda Jackson
50. Concorde

### QUIZ 21 London for experts

1. St Martin-in-the-Fields
2. Blackfriars and Blackhorse Road
3. The Charity Zone
4. Oliver Cromwell
5. Eros
6. Tabbies
7. A London bus
8. Bram Stoker
9. The Magna Carta of 1215
10. An asylum
11. Dover Street
12. Three
13. Brighton
14. 10°C
15. Bedlam
16. Charity
17. Bow Street
18. The Jubilee Line
19. King Edward II
20. Using the telegraph
21. The 296
22. King James II
23. The Tyburn
24. 1842
25. London bus driver
26. Camden Town
27. Cleopatra's Needle (approximately 1475 BC)
28. John Quincy Adams
29. 13
30. Christopher Marlowe
31. The Duke of York Column
32. St Ethelburga's
33. Barnardo's
34. Benjamin Franklin
35. The Clean Air Act
36. The 11th century
37. The West India Dock
38. The Cato Street Conspiracy
39. Jacob's Island in Bermondsey
40. The Peabody Trust
41. Charles Pearson
42. Thomas Cubitt
43. 6 million
44. Michael Caine
45. Lord Mayor of London
46. Down Street
47. Bedlam
48. Lambeth Palace
49. Whole Nut
50. Rules